The

Complete
Guide to
Sushi
&
Sashimi

The
Complete
Guide to
Sushi
&
Sashimi

Includes **625** step-by-step photographs

Jeffrey Elliot & Robby Cook

Robert
ROSE

For complete cataloguing information, see page 306.

Disclaimer

The recipes in this book have been carefully tested by our kitchen and our
tasters. To the best of our knowledge, they are safe and nutritious for ordinary
use and users. For those people with food or other allergies, or who have special
food requirements or health issues, please read the suggested contents of each
recipe carefully and determine whether or not they may create a problem for you.
All recipes are used at the risk of the consumer.

We cannot be responsible for any hazards, loss or damage that may occur as
a result of any recipe use.

For those with special needs, allergies, requirements or health problems, in
the event of any doubt, please contact your medical adviser prior to the use
of any recipe.

Design and Production: Kevin Cockburn/PageWave Graphics Inc.
Senior Editor: Judith Finlayson
Recipe Editor: Tracy Bordian
Copy Editor, Proofreader and Indexer: Gillian Watts
Food Photography: Andrew Scrivani
Food Assistants: Devon Knight and Hugh Jernigan

Additional images: Utagawa Hiroshige (woodblock, page 11); © iStockphoto.com/
Alasdair Thomson (sesame seeds, page 28), © iStockphoto.com/Miyuki
Satake (yuzu, page 28); © iStockphoto.com/Alexandre Gibo (sudachi,
page 28); © iStockphoto.com/dinoforlena (eel, page 288); © iStockphoto.com/
LUNAMARINA (tuna, page 291); © iStockphoto.com/hdere (yellowtail, page 292).

Cover image: Assorted *nigiri* (page 147)

The publisher gratefully acknowledges the financial support of our publishing
program by the Government of Canada through the Canada Book Fund.

Published by Robert Rose Inc.
120 Eglinton Avenue East, Suite 800, Toronto, Ontario, Canada M4P 1E2
Tel: (416) 322-6552 Fax: (416) 322-6936
www.robertrose.ca

Printed and bound in China

3 4 5 6 7 8 9 LEO 23 22 21 20 19

For H and P, my future fishermen
—Jeffrey

For my wife, Mio;
my parents, Steve and Patty;
and my sister, Nicole
—Robby

Contents

The Basics

The Story of Sushi

MAKING SUSHI is deceptively simple. After all, it's just rice, vinegar, seaweed and raw fish. Yet here we are, at the start of an entire book based on that short list of ingredients. In truth, learning to make sushi is very easy, but mastery is another story. It comes only with time and repetition. Sushi chefs-in-training may dedicate several years to perfecting sushi rice before they are allowed to touch fish. But don't let that dissuade you. With a little practice you can make sushi at home. Developing a sound foundation of the traditions and techniques (of which sushi has many) will set you on your way to success.

The Japanese believe that all five senses should be in play when eating. Sushi is the epitome of this principle: You begin eating sushi with your eyes—the plate laid out artfully, the colors specifically arranged. Then, as you bite into a hand roll, you hear the crunch of fresh nori. The fresh smells of the ocean and of the ginger and wasabi tickle your nose. As the textures of the nori, rice, fish, green onions and sesame seeds play over your tongue and teeth, you taste their fresh flavors.

The Japanese are committed to seasonality. Done properly, combining fresh, seasonal fish and seafood with vinegared rice and little else creates a feast for the senses. Sushi chefs are often described as "artists" or "masters," having spent years honing their craft. Eating at the sushi bar is as much a performance as a meal, as sushi bars are the original open kitchens.

The story of sushi starts in Southeast Asia, is perfected in Japan, and is turned inside out in North America. Today sushi can be found from Anchorage to Zanzibar, made from ingredients never imagined in Japan. Sushi is at home in some of the most highly rated and most expensive restaurants in the world. It is also available at your corner store.

Contrary to popular belief in the West, the meaning of the word sushi *has nothing to do with fish. It relates to the sour taste of vinegared rice, which is interesting because in sushi's earliest days the rice was discarded. Today we associate sushi with freshness, but it was originally a means of preservation through fermentation.*

The Creation of Sushi

The original form of sushi, *narezushi*, made its way to Japan from Southeast Asia and/or China sometime after the 3rd century B.C.E. The fish was cleaned and salted, then stuffed with rice and packed in a barrel. The barrel was weighted down with a pickling stone and the fish was left to ferment for up to a year. In the process, the proteins of the fish broke down into their constituent amino acids, creating a umami-rich ingredient. Once the fish was properly fermented, the rice was discarded and the fish was rinsed off and served. This type of sushi is still made today near Lake Biwa in Japan, using carp from the lake. The smell is quite strong, and some say that it is an acquired taste.

The Rice Remains

The next step in the evolutionary process of sushi was *han-narezushi*. The fermenting process, which originally took from six months to a year, was shortened to one month. Instead of throwing away the rice, the sour-tasting grain (created by lactic acid fermentation) was consumed with the fish. *Han-narezushi*, which is still found today (also strong smelling and very much an acquired taste, although less so than *narezushi*), was the style of sushi consumed in Japan until the 14th century C.E.

Pressed in a Box

Sushi making then evolved from being pressed in a barrel for one month to being pressed in a bamboo box for a couple of hours or days. This type of sushi was called *hayazushi* or *hakozushi*. Cured, cooked or fermented fish was packed on top of vinegared rice and pressed in a small box. Vinegar was used to mimic the sourness of lactic fermentation. Vegetables or seaweed could be added as a layer in the middle of the rice. With the vinegar flavoring the rice rather than lactic fermentation, the finished product was palatable to a wider range of people. This type of sushi was consumed through the 18th century and today exists as *oshizushi* (see page 178).

Rice Balls

By the 1800s, Tokyo (then known as Edo) was already a large and bustling city, and

Bowl of Sushi by Utagawa Hiroshige

food stalls were becoming a popular option for feeding the harried throngs. A chef by the name of Hanaya Yohei is credited with creating the next type of sushi, *edomaezushi*, the precursor to the *nigiri* sushi (sliced fish with molded rice) that we eat today. Yohei figured out that he could make rice balls seasoned with vinegar and slap a piece of fish on top (the result was relatively large by today's standards). It was the equivalent of today's fast food and the idea caught on and spread quickly throughout Tokyo and Japan. Yohei was able to establish a restaurant and leave his food stall behind.

The Benefits of Refrigeration
The fish used in Tokyo came directly from Tokyo Bay. But refrigeration didn't exist in those days, so Yohei had to cook or cure his fish. The widespread adoption of refrigeration technology meant that around the turn of the 20th century, sushi chefs could use raw fish in their preparations. Prior to then, ingredients that we consider a delicacy, such as fatty tuna (*toro*), would be discarded because they turned rancid quickly. To this day, *nigiri* sushi is the most popular style of sushi in Japan.

Sushi Rolls
The origin of sushi rolls (*makizushi*) is less certain, though they seem to have materialized in the late 18th century. The earliest recorded mention of a roll comes from a 1776 Japanese cookbook; however, the wrapping is not seaweed. The recipe calls for a blowfish skin to be laid flat, topped with rice and fish, and rolled (using the skin as a wrap).

Nori (the dried seaweed used for sushi rolls) was not widely cultivated until the early 1950s, after a discovery by a British scientist named Kathleen Drew Baker that made production more reliable. Prior to this, nori was rare and expensive; *nigiri* was king. This is still the case in Japan: rolls are an afterthought, and *nigiri* is the star of the show. In North America, the opposite is the case, and this preference led to the next advancement.

Inside Out
The next big change in sushi didn't happen in Japan, but in California in the 1960s! At that time, the few Japanese restaurants that existed mainly served Japanese expat businessmen. It was difficult for the chefs to get the fatty tuna (*toro*) that their customers craved, so, according to one story, a chef decided to make a roll out of avocado to simulate the fat and texture of fatty tuna. This roll evolved to include the addition of cucumber and crab.

At some point someone had the brilliant idea of turning the roll inside out, by placing the rice on the outside. The nori, which was unfamiliar to Westerners, was hidden. Today we know this type of roll as *uramaki*; in particular it's called a California roll. This move is credited with the rapid spread of sushi's popularity across North America and eventually around the world. Today, the inside-out California roll is even served in Japan. This spawned a new era of creativity among sushi chefs. Today you will find ingredients in rolls that would never have been considered in Japan, such as bananas, cream cheese and smoked salmon.

Once sushi was a luxury item eaten outside of Japan only by wealthy Japanese businessmen. Today it is available everywhere from fine dining establishments to corner grocery stores and—after you've read this book—your own kitchen. Who knows, maybe the next step in the evolution of sushi will be made by you!

Ingredients

WHEN CONSUMING raw food, or cooked food for that matter, your ingredients must be the best available and at their peak of freshness, season and quality. Most Japanese ingredients can be found in any large supermarket, but some will have to be sought out at Asian or Japanese markets. Westerners have expanded the list of ingredients used in sushi to include foods such as avocado, salmon, carrots, peppers—the list is practically endless. When making sushi, especially rolls, you are limited only by your imagination, but it is best to develop a solid foundation in traditional ingredients and techniques before charging off on your own.

Rice

Rice is probably the single most important ingredient in the making of sushi. In fact, the word *sushi* refers to rice seasoned with vinegar, and not, as one might think, to fish. Sushi chefs may spend years mastering rice before they begin to cut fish.

Rice is a staple food in Japan. When visiting Japan, one of the things that will strike you is that any available land is occupied by rice paddies. The Japanese consume so much rice that it is difficult to obtain Japanese-produced rice outside of Japan. In addition, to protect the local industry, the Japanese government does not allow rice to be imported from outside the country.

All rice grown in Japan is of the Japonica variety, which is essential for making sushi rice (see page 143). Japonica is a medium-grain rice that appears stubby and fat. It is the best for making sushi rice because it is somewhat, but not overly, sticky.

Japonica rice has many cultivars. A cultivar is a plant variety that has been produced by selective breeding as opposed to genetic modification. The cultivar currently most popular for making sushi rice is *koshihikari*. It has a sweet, nutty taste and a translucent quality that many sushi chefs prefer.

Japanese chefs differentiate between "new-crop" or *shinmai* rice and "old-crop" or *komai* rice. *Shinmai* is sold in the same year that it is harvested, from fall to the end of the year. *Shinmai* has more moisture and is considered sweeter than *komai* and best eaten plain or lightly adorned. It also requires slightly less liquid when cooking. However, many sushi chefs consider *komai* better for making sushi. As the rice dries, tiny cracks appear in the grains. These crevices assist with vinegar absorption. In the fall, when *shinmai* is widely marketed, most sushi chefs will combine *shinmai* and *komai* to balance out the moisture level of the rice.

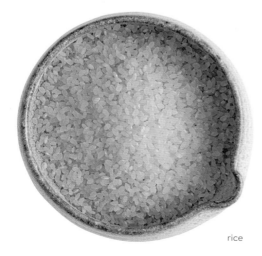

rice

Brown rice has become a popular choice for more health-conscious diners, especially in North America. White rice has been stripped of the outer layers of bran and germ, losing their inherent nutrients. Brown rice keeps the bran and germ, and therefore their nutritional value, intact. Because it maintains the outer layers, brown rice is harder and not as fluffy or sweet as white rice. This hardness makes it less sticky. It also makes it more difficult for the rice to absorb sushi vinegar. If you don't eat rice or sushi every day, we recommend using the traditional white sushi rice as an occasional indulgence. If you consume a lot of rice, you might consider using brown rice—just make sure it is the Japonica variety (*genmai*). For detailed information on preparing sushi rice, white or brown, see page 143.

Vinegar

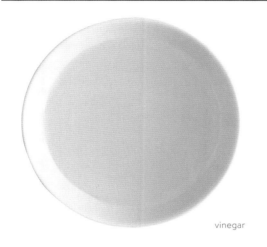

vinegar

Vinegar is called *su* (the *su* in sushi). In Japan it is always made from rice or sake lees (the leftovers from making sake). Japanese vinegars are mellower than many of their Western counterparts; their acidity is in the 4.5% range (distilled or cider vinegar typically has 5% acidity). Vinegar is important in sushi making because it is a key component of sushi rice. When making sushi rice, rice vinegar is seasoned with a combination of *konbu*, sugar, salt and sometimes sake or mirin. It is called *awasezu* (see recipe, page 141).

Soy Sauce

soy sauce

Soy sauce is originally from China. It is known as *shōyu* in Japan. The best Japanese *shōyus* take up to two years to make. Although the name implies that it is made from soy, *shōyu* is actually made from both soy and wheat in equal proportions. In traditionally made *shōyu*, boiled soybeans and roasted crushed wheat grains are combined with mold cultures from a beneficial type of fungus (aspergillus), which are either added or absorbed from the environment. This mixture is then mixed with coarse salt or salt brine and left to brew. This process breaks down the proteins in the beans and grains and facilitates fermentation.

Once the mixture is fully fermented, it is pressed to extract the liquid soy, which is then pasteurized and either bottled or aged. In Japan, *saishikomi shōyu*, which is twice-processed *shōyu* (after pressing, the soybean mixture is added back to the liquid for a second fermentation), is preferred for sushi and sashimi.

Tamari is a sauce that resembles *shōyu*. It contains little or no wheat but is instead the liquid by-product of miso production. It is a good alternative to soy if you need to avoid gluten, but be sure to read the label to confirm that it contains no gluten (some types of tamari do).

House Soy

Because all chefs have different tastes, recipes for house soy vary. We like the flavor of this version because it is neither too weak nor too strong.

MAKES ABOUT 3 CUPS (750 ML)

EQUIPMENT

- Fine-mesh sieve lined with cheesecloth
- Glass storage jar

TIPS

Use any kind of standard soy sauce in this recipe. Supermarket brands such as Kikkoman or Yamasa are fine.

This sauce can be stored in an airtight container in the refrigerator for up to a month.

½ cup	water, preferably filtered or spring	125 mL
2 cups	soy sauce (see Tips, left)	500 mL
½ cup	bonito flakes (*katsuobushi*)	125 mL
1	4-inch (10 cm) piece *konbu*, broken in half	1

1. In a small saucepan over medium heat, bring water to a boil.
2. Add soy sauce and return just to a boil (be sure not to let it boil or scorch on the side of the pan, as sauce will taste bitter and burnt).
3. Remove from heat and stir in bonito flakes. Set aside for at least 30 minutes or up to 1 hour to infuse bonito flavor.
4. Strain through prepared sieve into a large measuring cup.
5. Transfer to jar. Add *konbu* and tighten lid. Use immediately or refrigerate for up to a month.

Soy Sauces for Sushi

A sushi bar uses essentially four different types of sauces that are prepared from *shōyu*: house soy, nikiri soy sauce, light soy sauce and eel sauce. These reflect the preferences of the restaurant as well as the palates of the chefs. Each is for a different use, based on the kind of fish and the flavor the chef hopes to achieve. Three (the nikiri and light soy sauces, and the eel sauce) are used by the chef. A "house" soy is usually set on the sushi bar. (A sushi bar that serves only *omakase*-style meals or *nigiri* might not place soy on the bar. Each piece is brushed with sauce by the chef to suit the fish.)

Nikiri Soy Sauce

This type of soy sauce is brushed onto *nigiri* by the sushi chef before it is served. It is sometimes referred to as "dark soy" or "sweet soy." It is usually used for heavier, fattier and stronger-flavored fish, such as tuna, salmon, yellowtail or mackerel.

MAKES ABOUT 1¹⁄₂ CUPS (375 ML)

EQUIPMENT

- Glass storage jar

TIPS

Tamari is a more refined, yet more strongly flavored version of soy. If you prefer, use gluten-free tamari, which is often more readily available than versions containing gluten.

Adjust the quantities of mirin and sake to suit your preference.

If you prefer a sweeter flavor, increase the quantity of mirin. If you like the taste of sake, use more of it.

Nikiri sauce can be stored in an airtight container in the refrigerator for up to a year.

¹⁄₄ cup	mirin (see Tips, left)	60 mL
¹⁄₄ cup	sake (see Tips, left)	60 mL
¹⁄₂ cup	soy sauce	125 mL
¹⁄₂ cup	tamari (see Tips, left)	125 mL
1	4-inch (10 cm) piece *konbu*, broken in half	1

1. In a small saucepan, bring mirin and sake to a boil. Remove from heat. Using a match or a lighter, ignite and burn off alcohol.
2. Return saucepan to medium heat. Add soy sauce and tamari and heat until mixture begins to bubble.
3. Remove from heat. Add *konbu* and set aside until cool. Transfer liquid, with *konbu*, to jar and tighten lid. Use immediately or refrigerate for up to a year.

Light Soy Sauce

This version is lighter in flavor and color than regular soy sauce. It is used for leaner fish, such as fluke, snapper, stripe or bass, as well as for clams and squid. Lightening up the sauce allows you to taste the delicate flavors of these fish.

MAKES ABOUT 1½ CUPS (375 ML)

EQUIPMENT

• Glass storage jar

TIPS

Sudachi is a green Japanese citrus fruit. It is very sour and often used instead of vinegar.

Light soy sauce can be stored in an airtight container in the refrigerator for up to a year.

½ cup	sake	125 mL
1 cup	soy sauce	250 mL
1	whole lime, lemon or *sudachi* (see Tips, left), sliced	1
1	4-inch (10 cm) piece *konbu*, broken in half	1

1. In a small saucepan over medium heat, bring sake to a boil. Remove from heat. Using a match or a lighter, ignite and burn off alcohol.
2. Return saucepan to medium heat and add soy sauce. Heat just until mixture begins to bubble. Remove from heat. Add citrus and *konbu*.
3. Set aside until cool. Transfer liquid, with solids, to jar and tighten lid. Use immediately or refrigerate for up to a year.

There is an etiquette to using soy sauce when eating sushi or sashimi.

- *Soy sauce should be used sparingly. It is for dipping, not soaking your sushi or sashimi.*
- *When dipping nigiri sushi, do not soak the rice side in your soy sauce. This will cause the sushi rice to disintegrate, leaving the grains floating in your sauce. Turn the nigiri over to dip so that only the fish touches the soy sauce and turn it back over to eat.*
- *When eating rolled sushi, dip only a corner into the soy sauce. If submerged it will soak up too much soy and may fall apart. The flavors of the roll will be lost. This goes for gunkanmaki (battleship sushi) as well.*
- *Do not put wasabi in your soy sauce (see page 23). A good sushi chef will put wasabi on the rice for you in nigiri and in rolls. For sashimi dab a small bit of wasabi onto the fish if you prefer.*

Eel Sauce

This sauce is a reduced sweet soy mixture. It is usually brushed on freshwater eel (*unagi*), saltwater eel (*anago*) and eel avocado rolls. It is also used for other sushi bar items such as octopus (*tako*), abalone (*awabi*), steamed top neck clams (*hamaguri*) and squid (*ika*). Eel sauce takes time to make and requires attention. Prepared versions are available in most Asian supermarkets; they provide a quick and easy alternative.

MAKES ABOUT 3 CUPS (750 ML)

EQUIPMENT

- Wide deep saucepan (see Tips, left)
- Pastry brush
- Glass storage jar

TIPS

Using a wide saucepan will help to quicken the reduction period in Step 1.

Mizuame is a millet jelly that is similar to corn syrup. Look for it in Japanese grocery stores.

When the soy sauce, sake and mirin are simmering, use the pastry brush to wipe down the sides of the pan; otherwise, the mixture is likely to burn, which will make your sauce bitter.

This sauce will become much thicker upon refrigeration. Bring to room temperature before using.

1 cup	soy sauce	250 mL
1 cup	sake	250 mL
1 cup	mirin	250 mL
½ cup	tamari	125 mL
1 cup	granulated sugar	250 mL
¼ cup	*mizuame* (see Tips, left)	60 mL

1. In saucepan over medium heat, bring soy sauce, sake and mirin to a boil. Reduce heat to low and simmer until liquid is thick enough to coat the back of a spoon, about 1 hour.
2. Add tamari and whisk in sugar, then *mizuame*. Stir until sugar and *mizuame* dissolve.
3. Remove from heat and set aside to cool. Transfer to jar and tighten lid. Refrigerate for up to a year.

VARIATION

To produce an eel sauce with a particularly rich umami flavor, while reducing (Step 1), add eel bones, squid legs, octopus or scallops to the liquid. Strain (discarding solids), before cooling (Step 3).

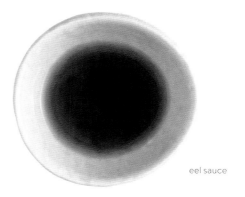

eel sauce

Japanese Rice Wines

Two kinds of Japanese "rice wines" are used when making sushi: sake and mirin.

sake

Sake: Although sake is classified as a rice wine, it is more closely related to beer, because it is made by brewing fermented rice. There are many types and grades of sake, from sweet to dry, and prices range widely. For cooking, use cooking sake. Look for it in well-stocked Japanese grocery stores. It is less expensive and its flavor profile is best suited to cooking.

Mirin: Mirin is made by combining glutinous rice and *shōchū* (a distilled spirit with similarities to vodka) and fermenting it for 2 months. Mirin is clear, lightly golden in color and very sweet. It has a pleasant aroma that is used to mask the smell of fish.

mirin

Sea Products

The most complementary flavors for raw fish and seafood are other flavors of the ocean. Seaweed—a major part of the Japanese diet—adds nutrients, texture and taste to many Japanese dishes.

Nori is the most common type of seaweed used in sushi. It is made from red algae, which is grown on ocean farms. Multiple harvests are generated from a single seeding. The nori made from the first harvest is called *shin-nori*; it is considered to be the finest quality. The best nori, in the opinion of most experts, is cultivated in the Ariake Sea off the island of Kyushu, Japan.

Nori is made in the same way as paper. The raw seaweed is finely chopped and mixed with water. This pulp is spread out to dry in thin sheets, which are cut and toasted. Nori attracts moisture and loses its crispness quickly. To maintain freshness it should be stored in an airtight container with a desiccant. Besides being used for various types of rolls, nori is used to wrap

nori

rice balls called *onigiri* or is shredded and used as a garnish and flavoring with noodles, rice or soup.

Konbu is an edible kelp grown in cold water. It is harvested in long strips (at least 3 yards/meters), which are then dried. The dried strips are sold whole or cut into smaller strips. In Japan, the *konbu* for dashi is cultivated near Hokkaido.

Konbu is important in sushi making because it is one of the three main ingredients in dashi (see below) and is often added to the water when making sushi rice or sushi vinegar.

konbu

Katsuobushi is smoked, dried and fermented bonito, a fish that belongs to the same family as tuna. In appearance *katsuobushi* resembles a piece of wood (*bushi* translates to "knot of wood"). The

process for making *katsuobushi* dates to the 17th century. The line-caught fish are filleted and simmered for a brief time to set the protein, then the pin bones are removed. Next the fillets are smoked for at least six hours a day for two or more weeks, using a variety of woods. At that point the fillets have lost most of their moisture and are set out in the sun to dry further (two to three days). Then the curing process begins. The fillets are laid out in chambers impregnated with the mold *Aspergillus glaucus*. After two weeks they are laid out in the sun to kill off the mold. This process is repeated for six weeks or longer.

Katsuobushi is the second essential ingredient in dashi (the third being water). For the best-tasting result, use the whole version, which is shaved on a *katsuobushi kezuriki* (see page 46). This device is similar to a wood plane mounted on a box with a drawer. Freshly shaved *katsuobushi* is preferable; once it is shaved it begins to lose flavor. However, most *katsuobushi* is bought bagged and pre-shaved.

katsuobushi

Dashi

Dashi is an essential stock that is used in many Japanese dishes. You are probably most likely to experience dashi in miso soup, as it is the base for that preparation.

The traditional way to make dashi is by steeping *konbu* and *katsuobushi* (bonito flakes) in water. This produces a complex, smoky, ocean-like stock. Nowadays—especially in home cooking—

dashi packets or powder (*hon dashi*) is used to speed up the process. The best dashi is made fresh, but if you are in a hurry, packets will suffice. Many different styles of dashi and many different kinds of dashi packets are available. Read the ingredients carefully to make sure what's in the packet conforms to your dietary needs.

Prepared Dashi

Some commonly available packaged forms of dashi are:

- *konbu* dashi—made from seaweed only
- bonito dashi—similar to traditional (*konbu*) dashi
- shiitake dashi—mushroom flavored
- *yasai* dashi—made from assorted vegetables
- *iwashi* dashi—made from dried sardines (more intense fishy flavor)
- *ebi* dashi—made from dried shrimp

dashi

Bonito Dashi

This method produces *ichiban* dashi. *Ichiban* means "number one" in Japanese. This is the first stock made from the *konbu* and bonito flakes. It is used for making miso soup, *nabe*/hot pots or other soup-based dishes. You can reuse your *konbu* and bonito flakes to make *niban* dashi. *Niban* means "number two" in Japanese because it is the second time the *konbu* and bonito is used. This produces a less flavorful and slightly cloudy version. *Niban* dashi is used in sauce preparations or for flavoring dishes that don't require a clear stock.

MAKES ABOUT 4 CUPS (1 L)

TIPS

For a more intense flavor, soak your *konbu* overnight, and use the liquid in the dashi.

When making dashi, it is important not to boil the stock. If you do, it will become cloudy.

Save the used *konbu* for making *niban* dashi (see above).

Cooked *konbu* can also be julienned and mixed with soy for a small snack, eaten with plain rice, or mixed into salads.

1	6-inches (15 cm) piece *konbu*, broken into thirds (see Tips, left)	1
4	cups cold water	1 L
1 cup	dried bonito flakes (*katsuobushi*)	250 mL

1. In a saucepan, combine *konbu* and water. Bring to a boil over low heat. As soon as the water begins to boil, use tongs to remove *konbu* and set aside (see Tips, left). Remove from heat.
2. Add bonito flakes and set aside to steep (off the heat) until the flakes sink to the bottom of the pot.
3. Once bonito has settled to the bottom, strain through prepared sieve to prevent any particles floating in your stock.

Keep the bonito leftover from making dashi for other preparations. It will have an appealing subtle flavor.

Wasabi

Wasabi is a type of horseradish (it is also known as Japanese horseradish). Wild wasabi grows high in the mountains of Japan in the water of shallow streams. Wasabi is also cultivated next to streams, and in rice paddies between planting seasons.

Fresh wasabi is very hard to find outside of Japan. Even in Japan it is a luxury. If you eat at a sushi bar that uses fresh wasabi, you are probably in a very good restaurant. The next best thing to fresh is fresh-frozen wasabi or grated wasabi found in a tube.

Wasabi is also available powdered and in a paste made from powder (packaged in a tube). However, some of these products are not actually made from real wasabi, so it is important to carefully read the ingredient list. Fake versions may consist of horseradish and/or mustard mixed with green food coloring.

If you are ordering sushi at a sushi bar, most *nigiri* sushi will already have a dab of wasabi between the rice and fish, applied by the sushi chef. The chef puts in the correct amount depending on the type of fish; a lean white fish will have less wasabi and a meatier fatty fish will have more wasabi. If you want to add more wasabi,

fresh wasabi

wasabi paste

add it directly to the fish or rolled sushi, not to the soy sauce. Adding wasabi to your soy will dilute the flavor of the wasabi. This way you can experience each flavor—fish, soy, rice and wasabi. If you really like wasabi, you can always ask the chef to add a bit more.

Daikon

daikon

Daikon is a mild white radish that resembles a giant carrot. In sushi it is used

pickled, shredded (julienned) or cut into long ribbons by *katsuramuki* (see page 24), in which case it can take the place of nori as a wrapper for sushi rolls. Daikon is also used finely grated in ponzu sauce (see recipe, page 27).

The sprouts of daikon radish, called *kaiware* in Japanese, are used as a garnish for *nigiri* or sashimi or in sushi rolls (*makizushi*).

KATSURAMUKI TECHNIQUE

If you've ever eaten at a sushi bar, you have probably watched in awe as a sushi chef deftly and effortlessly reduces a piece of daikon or cucumber to a single long ribbon. Although this is an entry-level technique, don't be fooled: this is one of the hardest cuts to master, and it requires a tremendous amount of repetition to learn.

The *katsuramuki* technique is used to cut long, paper-thin slices of daikon, some of which are used as a garnish for sashimi. The sheets of radish are then stacked and sliced into fine shreds (julienned). Once sliced, the radish is rinsed in cold running water to crisp. It is then used to garnish sashimi.

There is a machine that will do this (see page 46), but doing it by hand is a great skill to have. Like turnip, daikon is a hard vegetable, so make sure your knife is very sharp before starting

A *usuba* (see page 41) is designed for this task. However, you can also use a chef's knife, *santoku*, *kirutske* or *nakiri* (see page 44). Some chefs may even use a *yanagiba*, but the *usuba* is the best choice because this is what it was designed to do. Vegetable ribbons can be used as an alternative to nori when making sushi rolls (see page 271) or can be julienned and used as a garnish.

Katsuramuki-Cut Daikon

Before starting to peel the daikon, cut it into cylinders 3 to 4 inches (7.5 to 10 cm) long. When you are learning this cut, it may be easier to start with a shorter (2-inch/5 cm) piece. You can also cut it into sections and pare the sections with your knife prior to starting the *katsuramuki* technique.

▲ Grasp the daikon in your guide hand (see page 155), with your thumb on the front of the cylinder, halfway between and parallel to the ends, and the remaining four fingers behind. The top should be tilted away from you at a 45-degree angle.

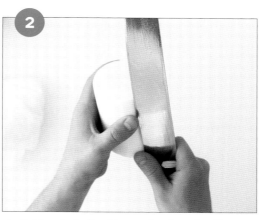

▲ Holding the knife with your thumb on the side of the blade closest to you, your index finger curved on the other side of the blade and your remaining three fingers around the handle (this is commonly referred to as the "pinch grip"), make a shallow cut into the side of the cylinder.

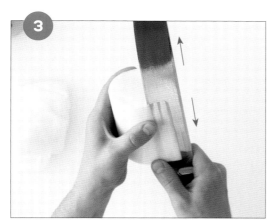

▲ Keeping the blade parallel to and flush against the cylinder, begin to rotate the cylinder toward the blade, using the thumb of your guide hand while simultaneously shimmying the knife up and down with the thumb and forefinger of your knife hand.

▲ Continue Step 3 until you are left with a small cylinder and a long ribbon.

Shiso

Shiso, also known as perilla, is an herb that belongs to the mint family. It is highly aromatic and has the flavor of spearmint and basil. Whole green leaves are used as a garnish (to be eaten) on sashimi plates. The flowers are used to garnish *nigiri* and sashimi. You may also find red shiso in some markets.

shiso

CHOPSTICKS ETIQUETTE

Here are a few rules to follow when using chopsticks at the sushi bar:

- Do not rub your chopsticks together. This is insulting to the restaurant, as it implies that they use cheap chopsticks.
- When not using chopsticks, set them on the chopstick rest in front of you.
- Do not use them as drumsticks.
- It is considered bad luck to pass food from your chopsticks to another person's chopsticks. In the traditional Japanese funeral ceremony, family members use chopsticks to pass the cremated bones before placing them in a burial pot.
- If you are sharing a large platter of sushi and sashimi, it is polite to turn your chopsticks around before serving yourself or a guest, using the ends that don't go into your mouth.

When eating *nigiri* sushi with chopsticks, it is easiest to tip the piece onto its side and pick it up with one chopstick on the rice and one chopstick on the fish. This will hold them together. You want to do this as gently as possible so you don't break the piece apart. Follow the same guidelines as for eating with your fingers: dip the topping side into the soy sauce and then transfer it directly into your mouth in one bite.

If you are a beginner with chopsticks, the best way to eat sushi is with your fingers. You will have more control and probably make less of a mess. This will most likely impress the sushi chefs, since the most common way to eat sushi in Japan is with your fingers. Always eat sashimi with chopsticks.

fresh ginger

Ginger (*shōga* in Japanese) is the most common spice in Japanese cuisine. Ginger is used sliced, grated, julienned and pickled. Pickled ginger, which is used for sushi, is called *gari* (see below). It acts as a palate cleanser and aids digestion. Despite what you've seen, pickled ginger should not be pink; it should be the natural color of ginger—yellow. If it is pink, food coloring has been added.

If you are ordering sushi at a sushi bar, *nigiri* sushi and rolled sushi are served with pickled ginger (*gari*) on the side. Most times with sashimi, it isn't served. The ginger is meant to be a palate cleanser between bites of different types of sushi. It is not meant to be soaked in soy sauce or eaten on top of the sushi.

Sushi Ginger *Gari*

Pickled ginger is a traditional accompaniment to sushi.

MAKES ABOUT 2 CUPS (500 ML)

EQUIPMENT

- One pint (500 mL) preserving jar, with lid

TIPS

It is best to use young ginger, which is available in the early summer.

The ginger needs to marinate for at least 3 days to tame some of its bite.

gari

2	5-inch (12.5 cm) long pieces gingerroot (about 14 oz/425 g), peeled and washed	2
	Water	
	Salt	
1 cup	Japanese rice vinegar	250 mL
¾ cup	granulated sugar	175 mL

1. On a cutting board, using a chef's knife or *usuba*, cut ginger into very thin slices. (If you prefer, use a mandoline or peeler instead.)
2. In a large pot of boiling salted water, blanch ginger slices for 30 seconds. Drain and transfer to jar.
3. In a small saucepan, bring vinegar, 1 cup (250 mL) water, sugar and 1 tsp (5 mL) salt to a boil, stirring until the sugar is dissolved.
4. Pour over ginger, then tighten lid. Allow to cool to room temperature. Transfer to refrigerator and let marinate for at least 3 days (see Tips, left). Pickled ginger will keep in an airtight container in the refrigerator for up to a year.

Goma

Goma is the Japanese word for white and black sesame seeds, both of which are used in Japanese cuisine. They add visual appeal, texture and a slight nutty flavor to inside-out rolls, which is their most popular use in sushi. Sesame seeds are usually toasted before use.

goma

Kyūri

kyūri

Kyūri are Japanese "burpless" cucumbers (which means they don't contain the compound that causes bitterness and makes people burp after ingesting them). They are shorter and more slender than their Western counterparts, often only about 4 inches (10 cm) long. They are sweet and seedless, and the skin is edible. *Kyūri* are used for one of the most popular rolls in Japan: *kappamaki* (single-ingredient cucumber rolls). *Kyūri* are used as a component in other rolls, such as the Western California roll, and are also served pickled. If you can't find Japanese cucumbers, you can substitute Persian or English cucumbers.

Sasa

sasa

Sasa (bamboo leaf) is used in presentation —either whole or decoratively cut—as a base for food to rest on or to separate foods. *Sasa* can also be used as a wrapping for food. Early sushi was wrapped in *sasa* to help preserve it and to kill bacteria. The leaves have anti-microbial properties which reduce the risk of food poisoning.

Yuzu and *Sudachi*

Yuzu and *sudachi* are sour citrus fruits. Yuzu, which can be yellow or green, resemble small grapefruit. *Sudachi* are small, round and green, like key limes. Their juice can take the place of vinegar, especially in ponzu sauce (see page 29). The zest of the yuzu can be used as a garnish, and the juice is also used as a flavoring agent, similar to the way lemon juice is used in the West.

yuzu

sudachi

Ponzu

Ponzu is a citrus-flavored sauce. It is a very versatile sauce that you'll find uses for outside of sushi; for example, when mixed with oil, it makes a nice marinade or vinaigrette for grilled fish. In the Kansai region of Japan it is often served with sashimi.

MAKES ABOUT 2 CUPS (500 ML)

EQUIPMENT

• One quart (1 L) preserving jar, with lid

TIPS

Instead of lemon, you can use other citrus fruits, such as orange, lime and *sudachi*, in equal proportion.

Using a cheesecloth or paper towel to strain will prevent any bonito particles in your sauce.

1 cup	soy sauce	250 mL
1 cup	rice or ponzu vinegar	250 mL
⅓ cup	sake	75 mL
⅓ cup	mirin	75 mL
1	lemon, thinly sliced (see Tips, left)	
2	sheets (each 6 inches/15 cm) *konbu*, broken in half	2
1 cup	bonito flakes (*katsuobushi*; about ¼ oz/7 g)	250 mL

1. In a bowl, whisk together soy sauce, vinegar, sake and mirin. Add lemon, *konbu* and bonito and stir well. Cover and refrigerate overnight.
2. Strain into jar (see Tips, left), cover tightly and refrigerate for up to 1 month.

Tofu

Tofu is a fresh curd made from soy milk. It is a staple in Japanese cuisine and has many uses in a sushi kitchen. For instance, fried tofu is made into pockets and used to make *inarizushi* (page 278) and as a filling in sushi rolls. Freeze-dried tofu, called *kōyadōfu*, is reconstituted and used as a filling in sushi rolls. Cubed tofu is also used in miso soup.

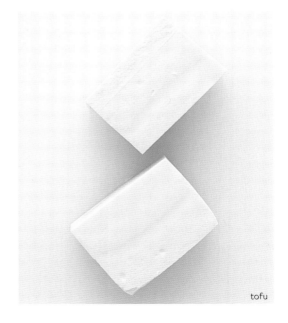

tofu

Miso Soup

Miso soup, which is ubiquitous in Japanese restaurants, is associated with sushi almost as much as rice and fish. This traditional accompaniment to sushi is quick and easy to make. Traditionally you eat the ingredients and then drink the broth from your bowl. This version uses dashi, but you can easily make it vegan by using vegetable or shiitake mushroom stock instead of traditional dashi.

MAKES
4 SERVINGS

EQUIPMENT

• Fine-mesh sieve, optional

TIPS

If you prefer a saltier soup, increase the quantity of miso.

Pushing the miso through a fine-mesh sieve ensures there will be no chunks in your soup.

2 tbsp	dried wakame	30 mL
4 cups	dashi (see page 22)	1 L
⅓ cup	red miso paste (see Tips, left)	75 mL
5 oz	silken tofu, cut into ½-inch (1 cm) cubes	150 g
2 tbsp	thinly sliced green onion, white and green parts	30 mL

1. Place wakame in a small bowl and cover with water. Set aside until wakame is soft, about 30 minutes. Drain, squeeze out excess water and set aside.
2. In a large saucepan, bring dashi just to a simmer (do not boil).
3. Place sieve (if using) in dashi and, using the back of a spoon, push miso into broth (see Tips, left). (If not using a sieve, stir miso into broth.) Whisk well until miso is dissolved.
4. Stir in tofu and reserved wakame and heat until warmed through.
5. Transfer to individual serving bowls and garnish with green onion. Serve immediately.

Japanese Mayonnaise

Japanese mayonnaise has a slightly different flavor and thinner consistency than classic French mayonnaise. It is typically made with apple cider vinegar, rice vinegar or malt vinegar, on their own or in combination, rather than distilled vinegar or lemon juice, which is found in Western mayonnaise. The addition of MSG also contributes to its distinctive flavor. Kewpie, the most popular brand of mayonnaise in Japan, has an almost cult-like following among chefs all over the world. It uses rice and malt vinegars and

Japanese mayo   spicy mayo

egg yolks rather than whole eggs, which is common in some types of commercially made mayonnaise. Mayonnaise spiked with chiles (see below) is used to make spicy tuna rolls (see recipe, page 217).

Spicy Mayo

Spicy mayonnaise is what adds the "spicy" to the very popular spicy tuna roll. You can use spicy mayo anywhere you would use plain mayonnaise, to add a little kick.

MAKES 1¼ CUPS (300 ML)

TIPS

Use your favorite mayonnaise—Kewpie, Hellman's or even homemade. If you are using Kewpie mayonnaise, make sure you are not serving it to anyone with a sensitivity to MSG.

Any Asian hot sauce or chile paste, such as Sriracha, sambal oelek, *tobanjan* or *kochujang*, works well in this recipe.

If you are heat sensitive, use less chile paste. If you are a heat seeker, increase the quantity or add the chili flakes.

1 cup	mayonnaise (see Tips, left)	250 mL
3 tbsp	chile paste (see Tips, left)	45 mL
1 tsp	Japanese toasted sesame oil	5 mL
1 tsp	freshly squeezed lemon juice	5 mL
	Japanese chili flakes, such as *ichimi* or *shichimi*, optional	

1. In a bowl, whisk together mayonnaise, chile paste, sesame oil and lemon juice, until combined. Add chili flakes to taste (if using). Use immediately or transfer to an airtight container and refrigerate for up to 1 month.

Eggs

Uzura no tamago (quail's eggs) are used in *gunkanmaki* (battleship-shaped *nigiri* with nori wrapped around the outside). A raw quail egg is broken over the top as a flavor enhancer and garnish. Chicken eggs are the basis of *tamagoyaki* (see below).

uzura no tamago

Rolled Omelet *Tamago*

This type of sweet omelet is seen at most sushi bars and is a staple of Japanese home-style breakfasts. You may also see it served in bento boxes or take out–style lunches. If it is not used for sushi or a bento box preparation or eaten for breakfast, *tamago* is usually served with grated daikon radish and a splash of soy sauce. Although *tamago* is not easy to make, practice will help you master the technique. The quality of a sushi bar can be judged by the quality of *tamagoyaki*.

MAKES 12 SERVINGS FOR SASHIMI, 24 SERVINGS FOR *NIGIRI*

EQUIPMENT

- Small *tamagoyaki* pan (see Tips, page 35)
- Fine-mesh sieve
- Chopsticks or spatula

TIP

This recipe is for a half-pan-style *tamagoyaki* pan. This pan can be found in most Japanese supermarkets or online. Nonstick versions are available.

¼ cup	dashi	60 mL
¼ cup	granulated sugar	60 mL
2 tbsp	sake	30 mL
2 tbsp	mirin	30 mL
½ tsp	Light Soy Sauce (page 18)	12 mL
Pinch	salt	Pinch
6	eggs	6
	Oil, for greasing	

> ### VARIATION
>
> Add 1 tbsp (15 mL) roasted seaweed flakes (*aonori*) to the egg mixture in Step 2.

▲ In a small saucepan, bring dashi, sugar, sake, mirin, soy sauce and salt to a boil, stirring until sugar and salt are dissolved. Remove from heat and set aside to cool.

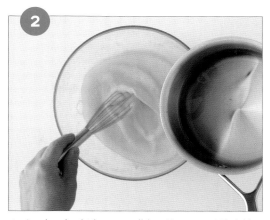

▲ In a bowl, whisk eggs well (see Tips, page 35). Add dashi mixture and whisk until incorporated.

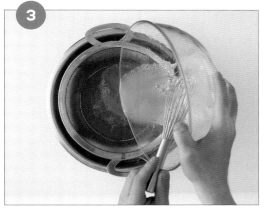

▲ Strain egg mixture into a bowl or measuring cup.

▲ Heat *tamagoyaki* pan over medium heat. Using chopsticks and a balled-up paper towel, lightly oil the pan. Set paper aside.

▲ Add about ⅓ cup (75 mL) of the egg mixture, tilting the pan so mixture is evenly distributed in a thin sheet that covers the entire pan.

▲ Cook until egg is just set but still a little wet on top. Use your chopsticks to pop any bubbles.

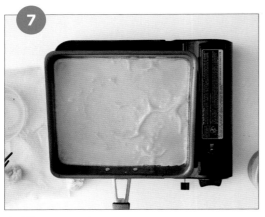

▲ Tilt pan toward you.

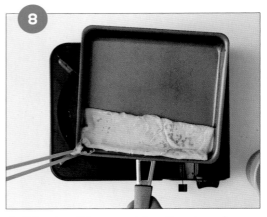

▲ Using chopsticks or a spatula, roll egg toward you (it should fold into thirds).

▲ Oil pan lightly, using the oiled paper towel.

▲ Slide cooked omelet to top of the pan. Add another ⅓ cup (75 mL) of the egg mixture, tilting the pan so it covers the entire surface.

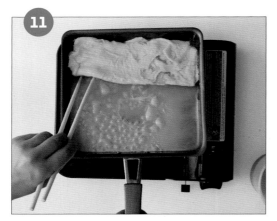

▲ Use chopsticks or a spatula to lift cooked omelet so some of the uncooked mixture can flow underneath. Repeat Steps 6, 7, 8, 9 and 10.

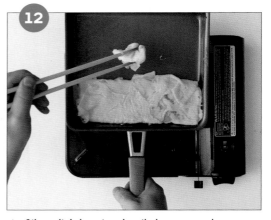

▲ Oil pan lightly, using the oiled paper towel.

▲ Repeat Step 10, then Steps 6 to 10, until you have used all of the remaining egg mixture.

▲ When egg mixture is used up and omelet is completely cooked, use a spatula to flatten sides into a rectangular shape (see Tips, below).

▲ Flip omelet onto a serving plate and let cool to room temperature, the ideal serving temperature.

TIPS

Small *tamago* pans are typically 6 inches (15 cm) wide and 6 to 8 inches (15 to 20 cm) long.

At the sushi bar we use a full-size pan to keep up with the demands of a busy restaurant. If you can find only a full-size pan, double the recipe.

Ball up and grease a few pieces of paper towel before starting. If your original ball gets dirty, discard it and use a new one.

If the eggs are not beaten enough you'll be able to see streaks of white in your omelet. You want it to be uniformly yellow.

Be sure to keep the heat at medium. If it is too low, the egg sheets are more likely to break apart when flipped.

The pan may come with a wooden lid that helps with shaping and flipping the omelet.

Remember to lift the cooked omelet so the egg mixture can slide underneath the growing omelet, adhere, and expand. With each fill and flip, your omelet will gain layers and grow in diameter.

Remember to oil the pan in between each ladle of egg mixture so that the omelet doesn't stick.

Pickles

In addition to pickled ginger (*gari*), various other types of pickles (*tsukemono* or "pickled things") are often served with sushi (see below). Some pickled vegetables are used as a filling for rolls (*makizushi*). You may also have seen something called *oshinko*, which is an assortment of pickled vegetables artistically sliced and plated and served as a side dish.

Pickled Vegetables for Sushi
- *gobō*: picked burdock root
- *kabu*: Japanese turnip
- *kanpyō*: soy-braised gourd strips
- *myōga*: pickled ginger shallot
- *nasu*: pickled Japanese eggplant
- *ni-shiitake*: soy-braised shiitake mushrooms
- *takuan*: pickled daikon

There are many pickling methods in Japan: salt (*shiozuke*), vinegar (*suzuke*), miso (*misozuke*), soy sauce (*shoyuzuke*), sake lees (*kasuzuke*) and rice bran (*nukazuke*). The first four methods can be easily replicated at home; the last two may require some effort to find the pickling mediums.

Most pickled vegetables can be found already prepared at Asian supermarkets. If you prefer to make your own, the recipe for *amazu* can be used with most vegetables.

oshinko

Quick Pickling Liquid *Amazu*

Amazu is used as a vinegary dressing for *sunomono*, a quick pickle of mixed vegetables dressed in sweet vinegar that serves as a palate cleanser and kind of salad.

MAKES ABOUT 2½ CUPS (625 ML)

TIP

Amazu is traditionally used with cucumbers but you can use this with other vegetables such as daikon and carrots. As a general rule, the denser the vegetable you want to pickle, the longer it should marinate in the *amazu*. Really dense vegetables, such as carrots, should be blanched first.

1 cup	Japanese rice vinegar	250 mL
1 cup	water	250 mL
⅔ cup	granulated sugar	150 mL
1 tsp	salt	5 mL
1	4-inch (10 cm) piece *konbu*, broken in half	1

1. In a saucepan, combine vinegar, water, sugar and salt and bring to a boil, stirring occasionally. When sugar has completely dissolved, remove pan from heat. Add *konbu* and set aside to cool.
2. Transfer to an airtight container and refrigerate for up to 6 months.

SUNOMONO

Cucumber Sunomono: To make enough to serve four people, thinly slice 2 Japanese cucumbers and toss with ¼ cup (60 mL) *amazu*. Divide among four small plates and garnish with a sprinkling of sesame seeds.

Carrot Sunomono: In a saucepan of boiling water, blanch 2 whole peeled carrots for several minutes, until al dente. Shock in a bowl of cold water to cool. Drain well and proceed as you would for Cucumber *Sunomono*.

Other Ingredients for Sushi

Meat (*niku*), both cooked and raw, is sometimes used in sushi. Beef from a breed of cattle called *wagyu* is used in *nigiri* and sashimi. *Wagyu* is known for its excessive marbling. *Torisashi* and *toriwasa* are types of chicken sashimi, with *toriwasa* being lightly seared and *torisashi* being totally raw. (Needless to say, the chicken must be of the highest quality. Chefs who serve chicken sashimi usually raise the chickens themselves so they can ensure the quality.) Western chefs have added other meats, such as foie gras (the fattened liver of ducks or geese), to sushi.

Other ingredients that can sometimes be found in a sushi kitchen are carrots, asparagus, green onions, bell peppers, cream cheese and eggs. In Western-style sushi your imagination is the only limit to the ingredients you can use.

Equipment

HAVING THE RIGHT EQUIPMENT is important to successfully making sushi. Although many standard kitchen implements are used to make sushi, much of what you need for a well-stocked sushi kitchen is unique to Japanese kitchens: single-edged knives, *hangiri, shamoji,* sharkskin graters, *katsuobushi* graters, sushi molds and *moribashi*, to name a few. This chapter will cover the basic equipment you need to prepare the sushi in this book.

Knives

The role of cutlery in the sushi kitchen cannot be overstated. When most people think of sushi chefs, they also think of knives. Knives are the most essential tools for making sushi. They can make the difference between good sushi and bad.

As chefs and admitted knife geeks, we own more knives than most people. We are also willing to spend a lot of money to get a knife that's to our liking, with a customized handle and finish. It's possible to spend thousands of dollars on a single

In Japan, left-handed knives are usually custom ordered and are much more expensive than right-handed knives. Often, chefs who are born lefties will retrain themselves to work with their right hand, for the rest of their lives or until they can afford left-handed knives. Sadly, sometimes this pressure to switch to working primarily with the less dominant hand is driven by a child's parents, who may be worried about the stigma of being different.

knife, but chances are only the most highly trained and skilled professionals can tell the differences (beyond aesthetic) between it and a knife that costs a few hundred dollars. These days a high-quality knife that will perform well and last a lifetime is available for between $100 and $400. A good knife should have both high initial sharpness and the ability to hold an edge for a long time.

Japanese knives are renowned the world over for their sharpness, which is reminiscent of samurai swords. Their sharpness is born of necessity: Raw ingredients are best consumed at the peak of freshness. When you cut something, you are damaging it, which speeds up the process of decomposition. You can slow deterioration by minimizing damage. In order to make the cleanest slice, traditional Japanese knives have only a single edge or bevel.

Single-edged knives are task-specific, meaning the angle of the bevel is designed to carry out a prescribed action, such as filleting a fish or slicing sashimi (the bevel on the knives acts as a guide, making their respective tasks easier to perform). For this reason, we recommend that if you plan to get serious about making sushi on a regular basis, you should buy and learn to use traditional Japanese knives. Traditional Japanese knives can be used for many applications beyond sushi making; for example, a *yanagiba* (see page 40) can slice roast beef as well as sashimi.

If a new set of knives is not within your budget, we have also included Western-style Japanese knives that are double-edged versions of single-edged knives, as well as Western/European knives that are designed for similar tasks, many of which you may already own and use (see pages 43 to 45).

Single- and Double-Edged Knives

As noted, single-edged knives make the cleanest cuts. When a knife has a single edge, it is either right- or left-handed, meaning that the cutting edge is on the right-hand side of the blade for right-handed people, and vice versa for lefties. Even double-edged knives in Japan (called Western-style knives) are ground to be left- or right-leaning. This is called "asymmetric grinding," and it is intended to produce knives that cause less damage while cutting. In the West, all knives are ground symmetrically (meaning they

are ambidextrous).

A store that specializes in Japanese knives will usually ask if you want a right- or left-handed knife. Stores that don't specialize in Japanese knives may not ask, so making that request is your responsibility. Many major Japanese knife manufacturers have started to grind their knives symmetrically if the knives are for import. When shopping for any knife, it's best to do your research beforehand and to be prepared to ask questions.

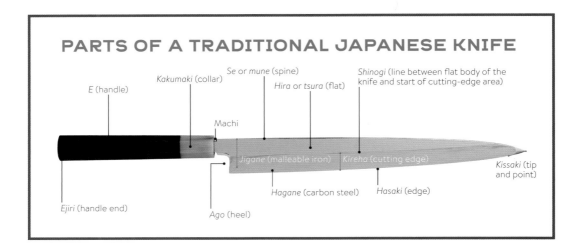

PARTS OF A TRADITIONAL JAPANESE KNIFE

E (handle)

Kakumaki (collar)

Se or *mune* (spine)

Hira or *tsura* (flat)

Shinogi (line between flat body of the knife and start of cutting-edge area)

Machi

Jigane (malleable iron)

Kireha (cutting edge)

Kissaki (tip and point)

Ejiri (handle end)

Ago (heel)

Hagane (carbon steel)

Hasaki (edge)

Traditional Japanese Knives

Traditional Japanese knives are manufactured in one of two ways, *honyaki* (which means "true-forged") or *kasumi* (which means "mist").

Honyaki knives are forged from one piece of very hard steel made by highly skilled craftsmen. It takes a chef to do these knives justice in terms of use and the care they require. Because the blades are so hard, they have great edge retention (*kirenaga* in Japanese). However, this hardness makes them more difficult to sharpen and easier to chip or break. These knives are for the aficionado and expert.

Kasumi knives are less expensive and easier to maintain than *honyaki* knives. For *kasumi*, softer iron is wrapped around a hard carbon steel core so that only the edge reveals the hard steel. *Kasumi* knives are great for beginners and experts alike. You can start and stay with these knives, or you can move on to *honyaki* knives when you are ready to care for and maintain them.

Traditional Japanese knives are often hyper-specialized for a specific task, such as the *usuba*, which is used for making ribbons out of tubular vegetables, or the *fugubiki*, which is used to cut poisonous blowfish.

Japanese knife handles usually come in one of three basic shapes: round, octagon or D-shaped, although these days handles can be made of any material and can be Western in style as well. Handle material and style are personal preferences and make no difference to cutting performance.

Japanese kitchens (both professional and domestic) use a mix of traditional single-edged Japanese knives and Western-style (double-edged) Japanese knives. For making sushi, we encourage you to acquire and use traditional knives to yield the best results; however, if you don't plan on making a lot of sushi, in the following pages we also suggest Western equivalents you can use instead.

Yanagiba

yanagiba

The *yanagiba* is the most recognizable traditional Japanese knife. Anyone who has been to a sushi bar has seen one. The name, which roughly translated means "willow blade," describes the shape of the blade: long and thin like a willow leaf. The *yanagiba* originated in the Kansai (Osaka) region of Japan and was designed solely to slice raw fish. Nowadays most sushi chefs can be spotted using as an all-purpose knife (similar to the way Western chefs use a French knife), julienning daikon, skinning fish or slicing sashimi and *maki* with one long, even stroke. The *yanagiba* is the most important knife for a sushi chef to own.

Deba

traditional deba

deba

kodeba

The *deba* is a thick, stiff, heavy triangular blade used to fillet and sever the head from fish. Its name is derived from its shape, which is reminiscent of a protruding (buck) tooth. The *deba*'s thin edge allows you to feel the bones of the fish clicking beneath the blade, and it yields an exceptionally clean fillet.

Deba come in a variety of sizes to suit different types of fish. Most chefs will have both a large *deba* for large fish and a smaller *deba*, called a *kodeba*, for smaller fish (*ko* means "small" in Japanese). Japanese chefs will also use a *deba* for some chopping.

Usuba

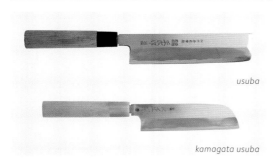

usuba

kamagata usuba

A Japanese adaptation of the Chinese cleaver, the *usuba* (which means "thin blade") is a thin rectangular single-edged blade. This knife is ideally suited to slicing vegetables, particularly when using the Japanese technique of *katsuramuki* (see page 24).

In the Kansai region of Japan they adapted the *usuba*, rounding the spine of the knife at the tip to make the *kamagata usuba*. Rounding the tip—and thereby removing some material—makes the tip lighter, facilitating its use in delicate and decorative cutting without bruising what is being cut.

Kirutske

kirutske

The *kirutske* is the closest thing to a multipurpose knife in traditional Japanese cutlery. A combination slicing and vegetable knife, it resembles a sword. Only someone highly skilled at using traditional Japanese knives should attempt to use this knife.

Hyper-Specialized Japanese Knives

Some Japanese knives are hyper-specialized and intended for use on only one type of fish. (It is unlikely that a home sushi chef would want to purchase any of these, but it is interesting to know about them.)

Fugubiki

fugubiki

A *fugubiki* (*fugu* puller) is a slicing knife that looks very much like a *yanagiba* but is thinner and more flexible. It was designed to yield translucent slices of blowfish (*fugu*), which is a poisonous fish. *Fugu* should be cut so thinly that you can see the design of the plate through the slices of fish. Sushi chefs must train for several years before they can safely slice *fugu*. Improperly sliced *fugu* results in about six deaths a year in Japan. Properly sliced *fugu* is supposed to contain just enough of the potentially deadly poison to cause a slight sense of euphoria.

Takobiki

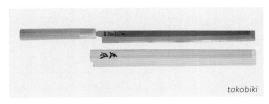

takobiki

The *takobiki* (octopus cutter) is popular in the Kanto region of Japan, which is known for its octopus. A *takobiki* is straighter than a *yanagiba*, and the tip is squared off so that while working the sushi chef is not pointing the tip of the knife toward the customer, which would be considered rude. (It is similar to a Western roast beef carving knife, which has a rounded tip as a safety measure because these knives are frequently used at buffet carving stations in front of customers.) Although a *takobiki* is specifically designed for cutting octopus, a *yanagiba* can be used to the same effect.

Unagisaki

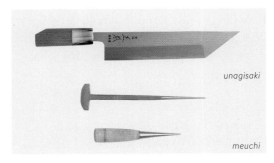

unagisaki

meuchi

The *unagisaki* (eel knife) is used to cut through the hard skin of eels. It resembles a *kiritsuke* (see page 41), but the front of the blade angles up to a sharp point rather than down. Often it is used in conjunction with a *meuchi* (eel spike), which is used to pin down a live eel. The point of the *unagisaki* is used to pierce the tough eel skin near the head, and then the blade is pulled down the length of the fish to separate the fillets. Unless you plan on filleting live eels, you probably don't need a *unagisaki*.

Maguro Kiri

maguro kiri

The *maguro kiri* (tuna knife) is the longest (up to 5 feet/1.5 meters) and most sword-like of the Japanese knives. It is used to fillet very large tuna because it can remove the fillets in one piece with a single cut. The longer *maguro kiri* sometimes requires two users: one to hold the handle and another to hold the end of the blade with a towel wrapped around it. This knife is rarely seen in restaurants and never in home kitchens.

Western/European Knives and Western-Style Japanese Knives

While we recommend that you learn how to use traditional Japanese knives that are designed for specific tasks when making sushi, Western/European knives and Western-style Japanese knives can be used to yield similar results. These knives will be double- rather than single-edged, will usually have Western handles and will be easier to use and maintain than traditional Japanese knives (see page 40); however, they do not have the precision sharpness that yields the best-looking and tastiest product.

These knives fall into three categories:

1. Japanese knives that are double-sided versions of traditional knives, as the *nakiri* is to the *usuba*;
2. Japanese versions of European knives, as the *gyutoh* is to the chef's knife; and
3. European knives, which can be used in similar ways to traditional Japanese knives, such as a fillet knife instead of a *deba*.

Chef's Knife and *Gyutoh*

gyutoh

The chef's knife, cook's knife or French knife is one of the most versatile knives in the Western kitchen. In a Japanese kitchen, the *gyutoh*—the Japanese version of a chef's knife, made with harder and thinner ground steel—can be just as useful. These knives can be used for filleting fish, cutting vegetables and slicing sashimi or sushi rolls. Either a *gyutoh* or a chef's knife can be used in place of a *yanagiba*, *deba* or *usuba* and produce more than adequate results; however, they will never do the job as well as the specialized Japanese knife.

Chef's knives and *gyutoh* knives range in size from 6 to 14 inches (15 to 35.5 cm). For preparing sushi, we recommend an 8- to 10-inch (20 to 25 cm) knife—the larger your knife is, the more you will be able to do with it.

Slicing/Carving Knife and *Sujihiki*

sujihiki

A slicing/carving knife is a long, thin, double-edged knife that can be used in place of a *yanagiba* if needed. The Japanese name for a slicing knife is *sujihiki*. When using one of these knives, cuts should be made in one fluid stroke. For working with sushi, a carving knife should be at least 8 inches (20 cm) long, but a longer blade, 10 or 12 inches (25 or 30 cm), is preferable so you can accommodate any size of fish. If your knife is too small, you may have to saw to slice through something, which will create an undesirable jagged edge.

Fillet Knife and *Deba*

fillet knife

A fillet knife, which looks like a traditional boning knife but is longer and more flexible, and a *deba* (see page 41) do not at first glance appear to be related. However, both are used for the same task: filleting fish. Where the *deba* is broad and stiff, the fillet knife is thin and flexible. Although Eastern and Western filleting methods are different, they can be accomplished using either knife. Filleting using a *deba* in the Japanese style (pages 64 and 74) will yield the cleanest results.

Nakiri

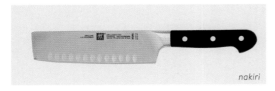

nakiri

The double-edged version of an *usuba* is a *nakiri*. Like an *usuba*, a *nakiri* has a thin blade and rectangular shape. It, too, is designed for use solely on vegetables.

Other knives that can be used for vegetables are Chinese cleavers, *santoku* knives, and chef's knives, although these have a little more flexibility in their usage beyond vegetables.

The santoku is a Japanese Western-style double-edged knife that resembles a kamagata usuba. Its name means "three virtues," which alludes to its use for cutting meat, fish or vegetables. While this knife is often found in Japanese households, it is rarely used in sushi restaurants. For a multi-purpose knife to use with sushi, the gyutoh, with its pointed tip, is better at slicing.

Petty Knives

petty knife

Petty knives are the paring knives of the Japanese kitchen. The advantage they have over paring knives, however, is in their greater length and breadth, which make them useful for accomplishing even more tasks, including filleting small fish (instead of using a *kodeba*).

Other Tools for Cutting

Kitchen Shears

kitchen shears

Kitchen shears can be used for a multitude of purposes in both Japanese and Western kitchens, such as cutting nori or *konbu* (seaweed), cutting the fins or gills from fish, or opening a fresh sea urchin.

Clam and Scallop Knives

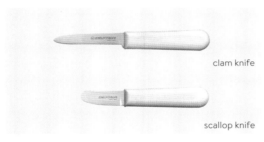
clam knife

scallop knife

Clam and scallop knives are stubby, rigid knives used for opening their associated bivalves. Clam knives are thin and have an edge on one side for wedging between tightly shut shells. The stiffness allows them to pop the hinges of the mollusk's shell. Scallop knives are shorter to keep from piercing the muscle. However, you can easily use a clam or fillet knife to open scallops, so it's not necessary to buy one just for the few times you'll be shucking scallops.

Mandoline

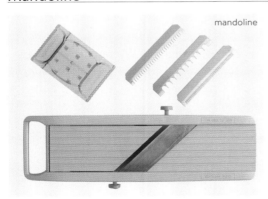
mandoline

A mandoline is a slicing tool that is used to quickly prepare vegetables. It can be used for julienning as well as for slicing vegetables. Inexpensive Japanese mandolines come with multiple blades and are razor sharp. Models with ceramic blades are also available. Ceramic blades will hold an edge for a long time.

Turning slicers

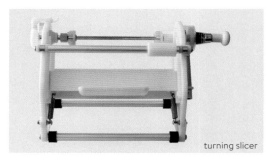

turning slicer

Turning slicers make an easy task of *katsuramuki* (see page 24), but a good one will likely set you back several hundred dollars. Note that there is more than one type of turning slicer for *katsuramuki*. Look for the kind where the length of what you're cutting presses against the blade, not against the end. Because they are expensive, we don't recommend buying one unless you plan to do a lot of *katsuramuki*. Spend the money on an *usuba* instead, which you can use for *katsuramuki* as well as other vegetable cuts.

Katsuobushi Kezuriki

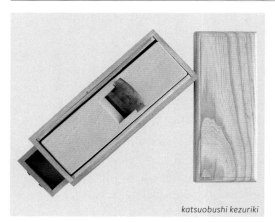

katsuobushi kezuriki

A *katsuobushi kezuriki* is similar to a wood plane and is used for shaving blocks of *katsuobushi* (dried, fermented and smoked bonito). *Katsuobushi* can be bought already shaved into flakes, but it is best when freshly shaved. A *katsuobushi kezuriki* shaves to the desired thickness and catches the flakes in a drawer below. Thicker flakes (called *kezurikatsuo*) are used for dashi, and thinner flakes (called *hanakatsuo*) are used as a topping and flavoring for many Japanese dishes.

Peelers

peelers

Peelers are often used instead of a knife for peeling fruits and vegetables, such as daikon and cucumber. Peelers come in either a straight or Y-shaped style and can have a fixed or pivoting blade. If you are not comfortable peeling with a knife, get a peeler.

Graters

oroshigane

samegawa oriskiki

Graters play an important role in the sushi kitchen. Sushi chefs use graters to break down the cells of ingredients such as daikon, ginger and wasabi to release their full flavor potential. Japanese graters differ from their Western counterparts in that they are not perforated; instead, the grated material collects on the surface of the grater. Ideally, you should have two graters: one for daikon and another for wasabi and ginger. Daikon requires the use of a coarser grater called an *oroshigane* ("grating metal"), which is usually made of steel or copper. Sharkskin-covered graters, called *samegawa orishiki*, are much finer than their metal counterparts and are ideal for breaking down the tough texture of wasabi and ginger. Ceramic graters, which are readily available, are a less expensive option for ginger and wasabi.

Urokotori

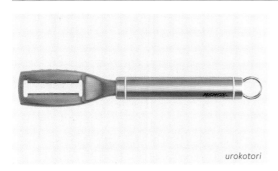

urokotori

An *urokotori* is a Japanese kitchen tool used to remove the scales from fish. You can also scale fish with the spine of a knife or a hard brush, but the *urokotori*'s design makes it very effective for the task. Traditionally, these utensils are made of brass, but they can also be made of steel (the material makes no difference to performance).

Fish Tweezers

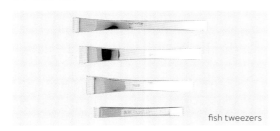

fish tweezers

Fish tweezers are an essential tool in the sushi kitchen. They are necessary for removing the pin bones from a fish fillet. Fish tweezers have wide, straight edges to make the task easier. (Just for the record, you cannot swap in a pair of cosmetic tweezers.)

Purchasing, Using and Caring for Knives

Good knives are expensive, and purchasing a set requires a significant investment; however, when handled, stored and cared for properly, your knives should last a lifetime. Japanese knives have become so prevalent that both traditional and Western-style Japanese knives can be found in most major chain stores, as well as in independent and specialty cooking stores. Do your research to identify quality manufacturers and shop around to get the best deal.

When purchasing a knife, make sure you hold it first and, if possible, cut something with it. The knife should be comfortable in your hand and feel like an extension of your arm. When you purchase a knife, buy a corresponding edge guard, sleeve or *saya* to protect the edge (*saya* is Japanese for "scabbard," which is a covering that protects the blade of a sword; it is most often made from wood and should be the exact size and shape necessary to cover the blade of your knife).

After using your knife, clean and dry both the blade and the handle to prevent spotting and rust. Even if your knife's packaging or manufacturer says that the knife is dishwasher safe, we don't recommend ever putting a knife in the dishwasher—the edge can get damaged and the handle can get discolored.

Store your knives in a way that protects both the edge and people from injuries. Knife blocks in which the blades go in sideways so that they don't rest on their edges, rolls and magnetic bars are all good storage options. Knives should not be stored loose in a drawer without edge guards or *sayas*, not only because collisions with other cutlery may damage the blades, but also because unsecured sharp blades are likely to cause injuries.

Good knives require regular care to maintain the sharpness of the edge. Traditional (single-edged) Japanese knives must be maintained by using a sharpening stone only, because the steel in them is harder than most honing steels. Western (double-edged) knives can be sharpened using machines or pull-through sharpeners, which are designed for double-edged blades, as well as stones.

Additionally, you can use a honing steel designed for Japanese knives (meaning that the metal in the honing steel is harder than the steel in your knife) for your double-edged Japanese knives, and any steel for your Western knives, to maintain them between sharpenings. If you have made an investment in good knives, we recommend getting a few quality whetstones and learning how to use them, which will give you much better control over the sharpness of your knives.

Sharpening a Single-Bevel Knife on a Water Stone

Water stones are easier and cleaner to use than oil stones. Professionals use a wide variety of grits, from coarse (for repairing knives and establishing an edge on new knives) to very fine (for finishing and smoothing the edge). The grit determines how much metal the stone will remove to make an edge, similar to the coarseness of sandpaper.

In some ways sharpening a single-edged knife is easier than sharpening a double-edged knife, as the *shinogi* line (the line that divides the side of the blade from the bevel; see page 40) provides a guide. Always follow the *shinogi* line: sometimes it is straight, but if it curves you will have to adjust while sharpening.

When sharpening, the stone should be perpendicular to the edge of your counter. You should stand as you would when you're cutting. In the directions that follow, we sharpen the knife in sections, starting at the heel and working toward the tip (depending on the size of the knife, this can be done in two to five sections).

TIPS

To sharpen and maintain your knives at home, we recommend that you have a minimum of one fine stone, with a grit from 2000 to 3000.

Before starting to sharpen your knife, soak your water stone for about 30 minutes (some synthetic stones don't require presoaking, just wetting).

If your stone does not have a base to keep it stable, rest it on a damp towel.

Even though double-sided knives can be sharpened with machine and pull-through sharpeners, we recommend sharpening stones for the best results!

To sharpen a double-sided knife, once you complete Step 9, go back to the beginning and repeat Steps 1 to 9 for the other side of the knife. You can either flip over the blade to the other side or switch the handle to your guide hand.

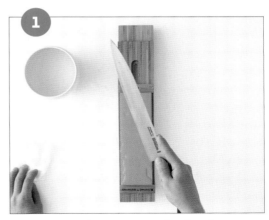

▲ Grasp the knife in your cutting hand, with your thumb on the backside of the blade near the heel and your index finger extended along the spine.

TIP

Regardless of the type of stone, you will need to work near a water source or have water available, as the stone will need to be wetted repeatedly.

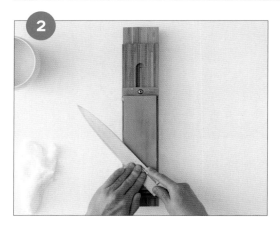

◀ Place the knife, edge-side down, near the bottom of the stone. The first section that you sharpen should be in contact with the stone, with the tip between 10 and 11 o'clock, and the bottom of the section near the bottom corner of the stone. The blade path (*kireha*), the area of the blade between the *shinogi* line and the edge, should be touching the stone. Place the three middle fingers of your guide hand on the back of the section that you're sharpening. Apply between 5 and 10 pounds of pressure. To feel what this is like, try pressing the knife against a kitchen or postal scale.

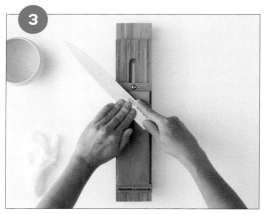

▲ While applying pressure, move the knife from the bottom of the stone to the top.

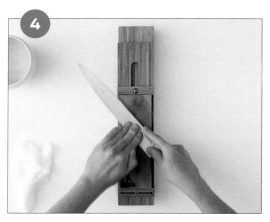

▲ Release the pressure and pull the knife back down to the bottom of the stone.

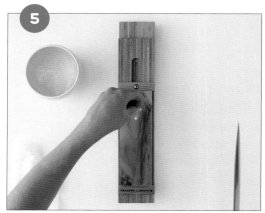

▲ Swiftly repeat Steps 3 and 4 about 10 times, pausing occasionally to check the edge and rewet the stone. You are checking the edge to see if a burr (*kaeri*) is forming. You do this by dragging the pad of your thumb down across the edge of the blade (you should feel a slight catching as the burr forms).

▲ Once the burr has formed, reposition the knife on the stone and your guide hand on the second section of the knife.

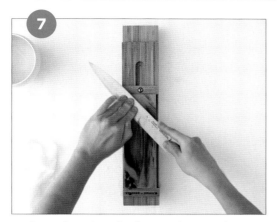

▲ Repeat Steps 3 to 5 for the second section of the knife.

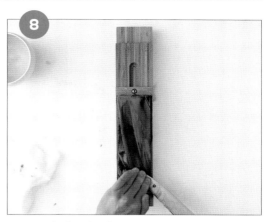

▲ Once the burr has formed on the second section, reposition the knife on the stone and your guide hand on the third section of the knife.

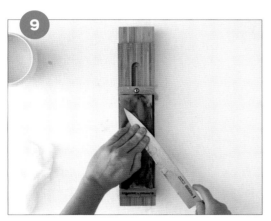

▲ Repeat Steps 3 to 5 for the next section of the knife. Keep repeating the steps until you've created a burr from the tip to the heel of the knife.

▲ Flip the knife over, placing the thumb of your knife hand on the spine of the blade, and the three middle fingers of your guide hand on the edge of the blade.

▲ Repeat Steps 4 to 10 until the burr is removed.

▲ A small burr will have formed on the flat side. Flip the knife over to the edge side and give a stroke or two on each section to remove the burr.

Cutting Boards

hinoki

A good cutting board is an important piece of equipment when preparing sushi. Cutting boards are made from various materials, but wood or plastic is preferred. Plastic boards are easy to clean and can be color-coded to the ingredients they are used for (blue for fish, red for meat and so on). However, perhaps surprisingly, wooden boards are more sanitary than plastic. Bacteria sink into and become trapped in the wood; bacteria remain on top of plastic boards, where they are more likely to contaminate your food.

Wooden boards come in *edge grain* and *end grain*. End grain is preferable, as it is easier on the edge of the knife because the blade passes between the fibers.

In Japan, *hinoki* wood (*hinoki* is a type of cypress) is often used to make cutting boards (as well as *sayas*/knife sheaths). *Hinoki* is renowned for its antibacterial, antifungal and quick-drying properties, so the best boards are made from it.

Plastic cutting boards can be cleaned in the dishwasher, but never put wooden boards in the dishwasher—they will warp and split. Use soap and hot water to clean your wooden boards. If your board needs a deep cleaning, make a paste out of coarse salt and water, spread it on the board and let it sit for a few hours or overnight. Scrape off the salt and wash with soap and water. This method is especially good for removing stubborn smells from a board.

It's a good idea to buy the largest cutting board that you can store and that will accommodate the largest fish you can imagine cutting. It's also nice to have some small boards for small tasks.

Rolling Mat (*Makisu*)

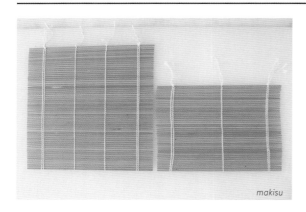
makisu

You will need to purchase a *makisu* (mat) for making sushi rolls (*makizushi*). *Makisu* are woven from bamboo and cotton string. The bamboo pieces can be either thick or thin. For sushi, the mats made with thin pieces of bamboo are best. Synthetic mats are also available, but bamboo mats are inexpensive and provide a great result. After use, mats must be thoroughly washed with hot water and soap and dried to prevent bacteria growth.

Tamago Pan (*Makiyakinabe*)

makiyakinabe

If you plan on making *tamago* (Japanese rolled omelet; see page 32), you will need to invest in a *makiyakinabe*, a square or rectangular pan designed to achieve the omelet's rectangular shape. Traditional *tamago* pans are made of cast iron or copper, and they must be properly seasoned prior to being used. Inexpensive nonstick pans, which do not require seasoning, are available at Japanese grocers. Because they are nonstick, these pans are easier for beginners to use and are an appropriate choice if you don't plan to make a lot of *tamago*.

Rice Cooker

rice cooker

You can cook rice in a pan on the stove, but for the best and most consistent results, use an electric rice cooker, a fixture in many Japanese and other Asian homes. Most rice cookers—especially Japanese rice cookers—have settings for sushi rice that guarantee perfect rice every time.

Rice cookers are available in either conventional electric or induction models. Some are pressurized to speed the cooking process. Most rice cookers have volume markers on the inside that indicate how much water to add for different amounts of rice. Rice cookers can also be used for cooking ingredients other than rice (for example, oatmeal and other grains such as barley), and some can even be used to make yogurt.

Hangiri and Shamoji

hangiri

shamoji

Once your rice is cooked and you are ready to make sushi rice, you will need a shallow bowl that is large enough to facilitate folding and cutting the rice. You can use any bowl that fits these criteria, but for the best results use a Japanese *hangiri*, which is specifically made for mixing sushi rice. This large wooden tub-like vessel looks like the bottom of a barrel. The wide surface area lets you cool down the rice and incorporate the vinegar quickly.

A *shamoji* is a flat spatula used to stir, serve and mix vinegar into sushi rice. Its wide, flat, stiff head helps it to accomplish these tasks better than other tools. It is traditionally made from bamboo or other woods, but *shamoji* are also available in plastic (in fact, most rice cookers come with one). Wooden *shamoji* need to be soaked in water before use to help prevent sticking; the plastic ones are less likely to stick.

When making sushi rice, you may want to use a paper fan to fan the rice to help cool it. Note that a rolled-up newspaper works just as well.

Plating Chopsticks (*Moribashi*)

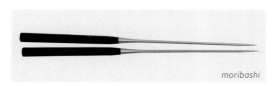

moribashi

Moribashi, or Japanese plating chopsticks, have been used by chefs in Japan for hundreds of years for delicate plating, such as adding fine garnishes to sushi or sashimi or arranging the fish on sushi rice for *chirashi*. Unlike the wooden chopsticks you eat with, *moribashi* are usually metal with wooden handles and have thin, sharp points that are perfect for fine and delicate work. In the West, plating tweezers are often used instead.

Pressed Sushi Box (*Oshizushihako*)

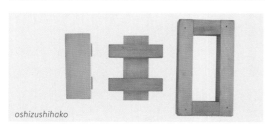

oshizushihako

If you are making box-pressed sushi (*oshizushi*; see pages 178 to 183), you will need a special mold called an *oshizushihako*, which literally translates as "pressed sushi box." The box (*hako*) comes in three pieces: a top, a bottom and sides. Traditionally the boxes are wooden, but they are now more commonly made of durable plastic, to which sushi rice is less likely to stick. Wooden boxes require soaking before use to help prevent sticking.

Fish and Seafood: Buying, Storing and Butchering

FRESH FISH is the foundation of good sushi. The best way to ensure that your fish is fresh is to catch it yourself. If this isn't an option, your next best option is to find a fishmonger or market that is clean and trustworthy and sells sustainable fish and seafood. Your senses are your most important tool when buying fresh fish and seafood—sight, smell and touch will tell you everything you need to know. If a fish market smells fishy, foul or ammonia-like, turn around and walk out. The same goes for cleanliness: if a store doesn't look clean, leave. Seek out fishmongers who have a good reputation and whose stock has a high level of turnover. Look for knowledgeable staff who can answer your questions, such as where and when the fish were caught.

Buying and Storing Fish

A whole fish should smell fresh, like the ocean. Its skin should be shiny and taut; if it's dull or faded, pass on it. When pressed, the flesh of the fish should spring back. The gills should be bright red, not brown. If the fish's scales are still on, they should be tight and not look dried out. Look for bright, clear eyes; sunken, cloudy eyes are a sure sign of an old fish.

If you are buying fillets, the meat should appear fresh and bright, not dull or discolored. Pay close attention to where the fillets were cut; if there are any signs of discoloration or drying, they are getting old.

Use Promptly and Store Properly

For sushi, you should use fish as soon as possible after you purchase it. If you need to store the fish, follow these rules:

- A whole fish will stay fresher longer than a fillet, so whenever possible buy your fish whole.
- Try to use the fish within 24 hours of purchase.

- *To store whole fish:* Fill a container with ice (ideally, crushed ice) and lay the fish lengthwise on the ice, right side down and with the head facing left (this is how they do it in Japan, so only one side touches the ice).
- *To store fillets:* Wrap fillets first in paper towels, to absorb any liquid that may be released, and then in plastic wrap. Place on a bed of ice (the wrapping is important to keep the fillet from coming in direct contact with the ice and getting a "cold burn"). Alternatively, you can place the fillet in a container resting on a bed of ice.
- There may be times when you need to freeze fish, such as when you have purchased too much. Freezing is also a good way to kill off parasites (see page 286). To freeze fish, wrap in a double layer of plastic wrap and then place in a resealable freezer bag. To defrost, let rest overnight in the fridge, or place the bag containing the fish in a bowl under cold running water until thawed.

Buying and Storing Seafood

Shrimp (*ebi*) are rarely sold live or fresh; if you can find any, you are very lucky. Previously frozen shrimp should be firm and fresh-smelling.

If you are buying clams (*aoyagi*), oysters (*kaiki*) or live scallops (*hotate*), look for ones that are partially opened but close when tapped. Ones with shells that are cracked or that won't shut should be discarded. Store clams and oysters on ice in a container with drainage holes so they don't sit in water. A colander set inside a bowl will work, but do not cover it, or you will suffocate the shellfish. Refrigerate and use within a day or two, draining the water and replacing the ice as needed.

Live crabs (*kani*) and sea urchins (*uni*) should be moving. Place crabs in a container, cover loosely with wet seaweed or newspaper, and refrigerate; use within a day or two. Most live sea urchins can be stored on ice for a couple of days. *Uni* out of the shell should be refrigerated on a tray over ice. *Uni* should give off a fresh ocean smell and appear dry; if a sea urchin looks as if it is melting, it should be discarded.

Squid is most often bought frozen. If you are lucky enough to find fresh squid, store it in a loosely sealed bag on ice until you are ready to use it (for one or two days at most). To thaw frozen squid, place it in a bowl in the fridge overnight; alternatively, you can put it in a colander under cool running water.

Japanese versus Western-Style Fish Butchery

The techniques for butchering fish differ between Japan and Western countries. This is in large part because of the different designs of the knives used to fillet fish. Western filleting knives are long, thin, extremely flexible and typically 7 to 7½ inches (about 19 cm) long (see page 44). Japanese *debas* are broad and stiff; they come in small, medium and large sizes, to tackle any size of fish (see page 41).

When filleting in the Western style, the knife is inserted at the back of the fish and the knife moves over the spine and out the belly side. When filleting in the Japanese style, the *deba* is inserted at the back or the belly of the fish and the fillet is cut away up to the spine; the process is then repeated from the other side. Only then is the fillet separated from the spine.

While we don't expect you to buy a *deba*, we do recommend it—using one will yield a cleaner fillet with less waste.

The Japanese have a quick method for filleting fish that is similar to the Western style, called daimyo oroshi. *However, this method is considered to leave too much meat on the bones, hence the name—the* daimyo *were feudal lords known for excess and waste.*

In this chapter we illustrate how to fillet both roundfish and flatfish using Western and Japanese techniques. Roundfish are fish whose cross-sections are basically circular (tuna, salmon, mackerel and amberjack fall into this category). Flatfish are literally fish that are flat, with both eyes on one side of the head (flounder, fluke and halibut, for example).

We also explain how to prepare shrimp, scallops, clams, sea urchins and squid for sushi and sashimi.

Japanese filleting methods are named for how many pieces they create. Filleting a round fish yields three pieces—two fillets and a carcass—so it is called sanmai oroshi, *or "three-piece filleting." Filleting a flatfish yields five pieces—four fillets and a carcass—so it is called* gomai oroshi, *or "five-piece filleting."*

Roundfish

Head Gills Dorsal fin Lateral line Adipose fin Tail

Pectoral fin Pelvic fin Anal fin

Flatfish

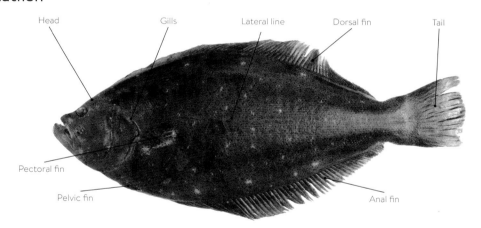

Head Gills Lateral line Dorsal fin Tail

Pectoral fin

Pelvic fin Anal fin

Cleaning, Scaling and Gutting Fish (*Mizuarai*)

The Japanese lump cleaning, scaling and gutting fish into one category called *mizuarai*, which means "washing with water." Before starting to clean any fish, it is a good idea to cut off the dorsal fin, as its spines are often very sharp. A pair of kitchen shears is well suited to this task. While you have the shears out, you can cut off the pectoral fins and gills as well, or you can do this later with your knife.

The Japanese have a method for removing both the gills and guts of a fish at the same time. It's called tsubo-nuki. To do this, insert a pair of bamboo chopsticks into the fish's mouth, to just past the gills. Twist the chopsticks clockwise a few times, then use them to pull out the gills and guts through the mouth. This method works best with small fish.

Scaling Fish

Removing a fish's scales can create quite a mess, as the scales tend to fly off and land everywhere. Most fishmongers will do it for you if you ask, but have them do it only if you will be using the fish that day. In Japan it is customary to hold the fish by the head when scaling, but you can also hold it by the tail if you prefer. Just remember that you will be scraping against the scales, from tail to head.

EQUIPMENT

- *Urokotori* or large knife
- Kitchen towel

A urokotori makes scaling a fish a relatively simple task, even though it can be messy.

▲ Lay fish on its side, with the tail facing your knife hand.

▲ Using a small towel to protect your hand, hold the fish by the head near the gills. Beginning at the tail end, place *urokotori* or the spine of the knife against fish and pull in a straight line toward head to detach scales (they should fly off). Repeat in swift motions across surface of fish until all the scales have been removed.

▲ To see if you missed any scales, run your hand or the tip of a knife over the fish from tail to head (it should be smooth).

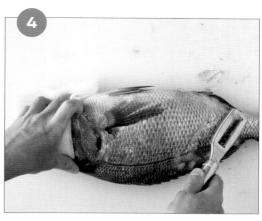

▲ Flip fish over and repeat Steps 2 and 3.

▲ Rinse fish under cool running water or in salted water (see Tips, below).

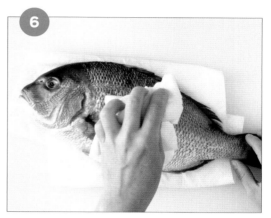

▲ Blot fish dry with paper towels or a kitchen towel.

TIPS

If you are scaling your fish at home, a good way to stay clean is to scale the fish in the sink or put it in a plastic bag to catch the scales as you work.

Instead of holding the fish under running water, some chefs rinse scaled fish in a basin of salted water (2 tbsp/30 mL salt per 4 cups/1 L water) to replicate seawater. This helps to maintain the natural flavor of the fish.

Cleaning Fish

Most whole fish that you buy from a fishmonger or grocer have already been gutted, but if you have one that isn't or you (or a friend) catch your own fish, here's how to do it.

EQUIPMENT

• *Deba,* filleting knife or chef's knife

If you go to a fishmonger in Japan, you'll notice that all the fish are arranged on crushed ice facing the same way: lying on their right side with the head to the left. The side that lies on the ice is considered slightly damaged and therefore less desirable than the other side. The right side is usually filleted first.

▲ On a cutting board, lay fish on its side with the head facing your guide hand and the belly facing you.

▲ Steady fish with your guide hand. Locate the anal fin (see page 57). With the edge of the blade facing the head, insert the tip of the knife about ¼ inch (0.5 cm) into the belly, just on the head side of the anal fin, taking care not to puncture any organs.

▲ Starting from the puncture point, slit the belly all the way up to the beginning of the head.

▲ Using your hand or the tip of the blade, pull out the organs and discard.

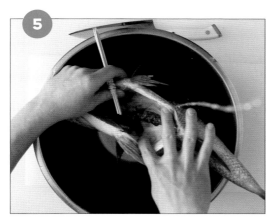

▲ Rinse the cavity of the fish under cool running water (see Tip, right). If any bits of organs still remain, use a toothbrush or other small brush to clean them out.

TIP

Instead of rinsing the cavity under the running water, some chefs rinse the fish in a basin of salted water (2 tbsp/30 mL salt per 4 cups/1 L water) to replicate seawater. This helps to maintain the natural flavor of the fish.

Removing the Head

In Japan, unless you are using the fish whole, the head is removed before filleting and reserved for another use, such as stocks, soups or sauces, or the head can be consumed on its own. Removing the head is the last step in *mizuarai*.

EQUIPMENT

- *Deba*, chef's knife or cleaver

The part of the fish right behind the head where the pectoral fin is attached is called the collar (kama) and is considered a delicacy when grilled. This is especially true of hamachi kama.

▲ Lay fish on cutting board with the head facing your guide hand and the belly facing you.

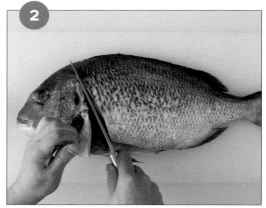

▲ Steady fish with your guide hand. Locate the pectoral fin (see page 57). Place your knife behind the pectoral fin, angling the tip about 45 degrees toward the back of the head and angling the edge toward the mouth. Carefully cut down through the belly to the spine.

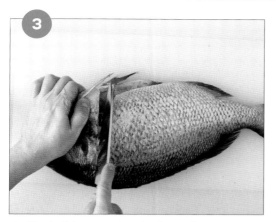

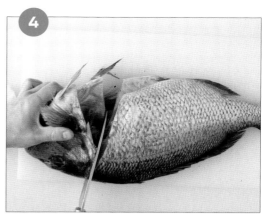

▲ Flip the fish over so the spine is now facing you. Place the tip of the knife just to the left of the pectoral fin, with the heel of the knife at the back of the head and the blade angled toward the mouth.

▲ Repeat Step 2.

▲ Using the heel of the knife, cut through the spine at the base of the head to sever it (discard head or reserve for another use). The fish is now ready to fillet.

TIPS

When butchering fish be careful of pectoral fins. They contain bacteria, which if poked, will cause your hand to swell.

When cutting through the head, you may want to place a towel on top of your knife and hit with the heel of your hand.

Save the head to make stock.

Three-piece Filleting
Sanmai Oroshi

Once *mizuarai* is completed and the head and tail has been removed, you are ready to fillet your fish. Here we illustrate three-piece filleting, or *sanmai oroshi*, which is used for round fish. (On pages 76 and 77 we illustrate Western filleting.)

EQUIPMENT

- *Deba*, filleting knife or chef's knife

TIP

Using a *deba* to fillet a fish produces the least amount of waste, as the angle of the blade allows you to feel your way across the bones. You can use either a filleting or chef's knife, but the results won't be as good. For smaller fish, you can use a *kodeba* or petty knife.

▲ Lay the fish across the cutting board with the head end facing your knife hand, the belly facing you and the head angled away from you.

TIP

If you are filleting a larger fish, it may be difficult to slide the knife all the way through where the vertebrae are thickest, nearest the head. If this is the case, use the tip of your knife to separate the meat.

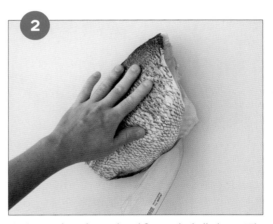

▲ Locate the pelvic and anal fins on the belly (page 57). Place your guide hand flat on the fish to keep it steady. With the index finger of your knife hand extended along the spine of the knife to guide the blade, align the edge of the knife just above the pelvic and anal fins. Cut the fish from head to tail, using as much of the blade as possible. Keep cutting in long, sweeping motions, without starts or stops, until you reach the spine.

▲ As you cut, use your guide hand to lift the fillet to help you judge the position of the blade. The blade should glide across the rib bones, and you should feel each individual bone as your blade sweeps across it.

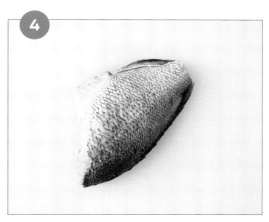

▲ Rotate the fish so the back is now facing you and the tail is angled away from you.

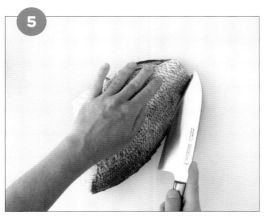

▲ Rest your guide hand on the fish. With your index finger extended along the spine of the knife, place the edge of the knife just above the dorsal fin and close to the tail.

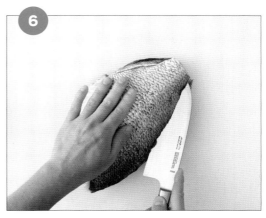

▲ Cut the fish from tail to head, using as much of the blade as possible.

◀ Keep slicing in long, sweeping motions, without starts or stops, until you reach the spine. As you cut, use your guide hand to lift the fillet to help you judge the position of the blade. At this point, both sides of the fillet—the belly and the backside—should be free from the ribs but still attached to the fish along the spine.

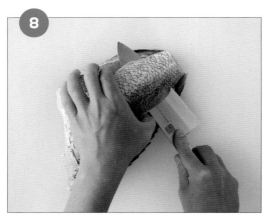

▲ Lift side of the fillet. Insert knife (edge facing tail) across the spine, separating a blade-width section of flesh from the spine, detaching fillet from the tail end.

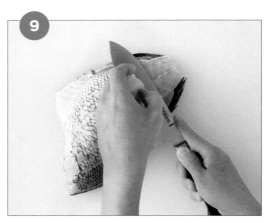

▲ Remove the knife and flip it so the edge faces the head. Hold the tail, reinsert the knife in the incision and slide it along the spine toward the head.

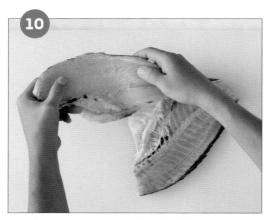

▲ After you have separated the fillet from the bone, carefully remove it and place skin side down on a tray lined with wax paper or on the cutting board.

▲ Flip over the fish and lay it on the board at an angle so the back is facing you and the head is facing away from you.

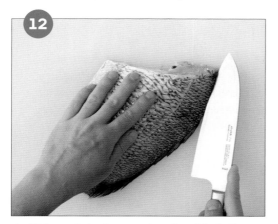

▲ With your index finger on the spine of the knife, place the edge of the knife just above the dorsal fin, near the head end of the fish.

▲ Cut the fish from head to tail, using as much of the blade as possible.

▲ Keep cutting in long, sweeping motions until you reach the spine. As you cut, use your guide hand to lift the fillet to help you judge the position of the blade.

▲ Rotate the fish so the belly is facing you and the tail is pointed diagonally away from you.

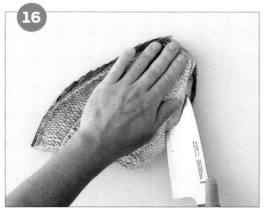

▲ Place the tip of the knife by the incision you've just made in the tail, then cut down to just above the anal fin.

▲ Keep cutting in long, sweeping motions until you reach the spine. As you cut, use your guide hand to lift the fillet to help you judge the position of the blade.

▲ Maintaining the position of the fish, lift the side of the fillet closest to you. With the knife edge facing the tail, insert the knife across the spine, separating a section of flesh the width of the blade from the spine.

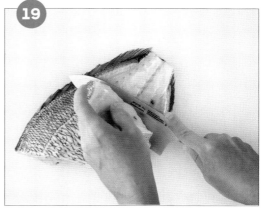

▲ Slide the tip of the blade along the spine, separating the second fillet to produce 2 fillets and the carcass. You are now ready to remove the rib and pin bones.

Removing the Rib Bones

This method will work with fish filleted in either the Japanese or the Western style.

EQUIPMENT

- *Deba*, filleting knife or chef's knife

▲ Lay fillet on the cutting board with belly side facing your guide hand.

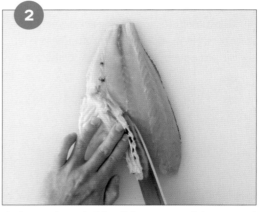

▲ Locate the end of the rib bones, toward the center of the fillet. Slide the knife under the length of the bones, then twist the blade slightly to lift the ends of the bones.

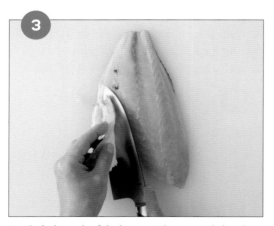

▲ Grab the ends of the bones with your guide hand, keeping the side of the knife blade flush against the ribs. Cut off the rib bones with one or two broad strokes, pulling them up with your guide hand as you go.

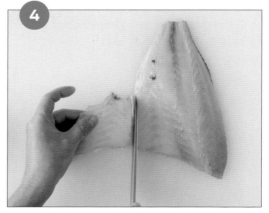

▲ When you reach the bottom of the fillet, cut away the bones completely and discard.

Removing the Pin Bones

Pin bones are the thin bones that run down the center of a fillet, with only their tips visible near the surface. This method for removing the pin bones works for fish filleted in either the Japanese or Western style.

EQUIPMENT

• Fish tweezers or needle-nose pliers

▲ Lay fish on cutting board with tail towards your guide hand.

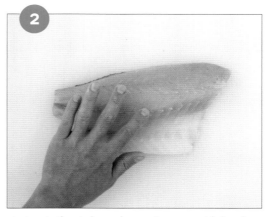

▲ Locate the pin bones by running your guide hand down the center of the fillet from the tail to the head.

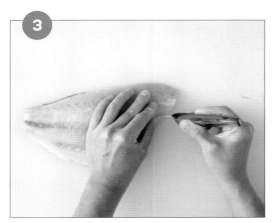

▲ Working with one pin bone at a time, grasp its end with the tweezers and then pull up and away from you to remove the bone.

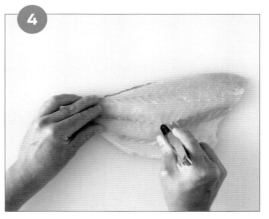

▲ Repeat until all the pin bones have been removed from each fillet.

Removing the Skin from a Fillet

Many types of fish can be eaten with their skin on, especially if they are cooked. But when eaten raw, most fish are preferred skinless.

EQUIPMENT

- *Deba*, chef's knife or filleting knife
- Slicing knife

It is easiest to remove the skin once the fish has been filleted, but some Japanese chefs like to peel the skin off a whole fish (particularly flatfish, because of their small scales); this technique is called sukibiki.

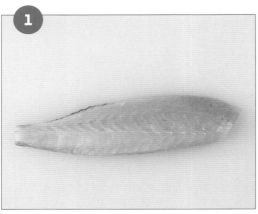

▲ Place fillet on cutting board, tail end facing your guide hand.

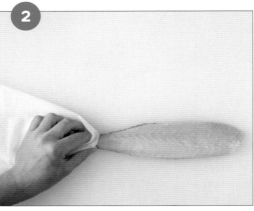

▲ With your guide hand, hold the tail end (use a small towel to help prevent slipping).

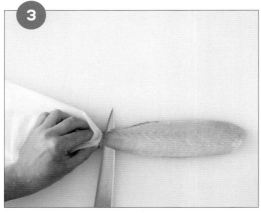

▲ Holding the knife at a shallow angle, as close to the tail as possible and with the edge toward the head, cut into the fillet down (but not through) the skin.

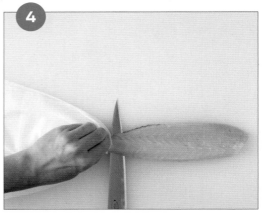

▲ Flatten the angle of the knife until it's almost parallel to the board.

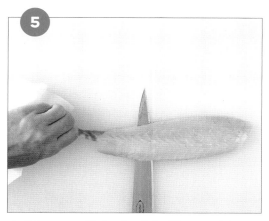

▲ Using your guide hand, pull the fillet toward the blade, simultaneously shimmying the knife back and forth and pushing it forward lightly, until the skin is removed.

▲ If any skin remains on the fillet, remove it with the tip of your knife.

TIP
Cut fillet in half down the lateral line to make it easier to skin.

SEARING FISH SKIN

Some fish you use for sushi and sashimi can be eaten with the skin on; however, you will need to sear the skin to make it less chewy and more palatable. There are two methods for searing fish skin. The first, which uses boiling water, is called *yubiki*. It is used mainly for snapper. Be aware that the larger the fish the chewier the skin will be. It is best to take the skin off larger snappers.

Yubiki **method:** Place fillet on a bamboo strainer or wire roasting rack tail side facing up. Place a wet cloth on top. Using a ladle or a smaller saucepan, pour boiling water on fillet from tail to head, making sure to cover all the skin with boiling water. Quickly transfer fillet to an ice bath. Let cool completely, then remove and pat dry with paper towels.

Tataki **method:** This involves searing the skin with a handheld torch. When using a blowtorch, it is best to place the fillet on top of crushed ice to prevent it from cooking.

Cleaning Flatfish

By virtue of their shape and anatomy, flatfish must be cleaned and filleted using a different approach than for roundfish. Flatfish don't have right and left sides but rather a colored top and a white bottom. The Eastern and Western methods are very similar, with just a few minor exceptions, so here we demonstrate only the *gomai oroshi* method.

EQUIPMENT

• *Deba* or filleting knife

To gut a flatfish, it is necessary to remove the head.

1

▲ Lay the fish on the cutting board with the head facing your guide hand and the belly facing you.

2

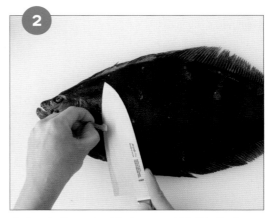

▲ Locate the pectoral fin (see page 57). Grip the fin with your guide hand and pull it outward. Using the knife, slice it off.

3

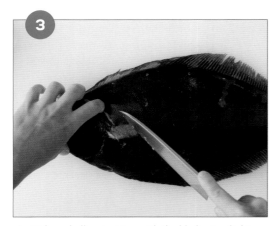

▲ Make a shallow incision with the blade at a slight angle, from just behind the top of the head to the pectoral fin continuing to the belly, to expose the organ cavity, taking care not to cut into the organs beneath.

4

▲ Flip over the fish so that the bottom (white) side is facing up, the back is toward you and the head is to the left. Repeat Step 2.

▲ Repeat Step 3.

▲ Put down the knife. Gently pull the head away from the body to expose the organs.

▲ Carefully grab the organs in your guide hand, then flip the fish over again so that the top (dark) side is facing up and the belly is facing you, with the head to the left.

▲ Still holding the organs in your guide hand, place the knife behind the pectoral fin and cut from the pectoral fin to the belly, completely severing the head from the body.

▲ Rinse the cavity under cool running water (see Tip, right), using a toothbrush or chopsticks to remove any remaining pieces of organs sticking to the cavity wall. The fish is now ready to fillet.

TIPS

Because their organs are very close to the head and rupturing the gallbladder can cause the fillets to taste bad, extra care must be taken to clean flatfish.

When cutting through the head, you may want to place a small towel on top of your knife and hit with the heel of your hand.

Instead of using running water, some chefs rinse scaled fish in a basin of salted water (2 tbsp/30 mL salt per 4 cups/ 1 L water) to replicate seawater, helping to maintain the natural flavor of the fish.

Flatfish: Five-Piece Filleting *Gomai Oroshi*

The shape of flatfish makes it easier to cut the meat into four fillets, versus the two fillets you get from a roundfish. Starting by making a shallow incision all the way around the fish makes it easier to remove the fillets.

EQUIPMENT

• *Deba* or filleting knife

TIP

Sometimes your fish will already have a shallow cut by the tail; this is how the fish was bled out.

🔺 Lay the fish on the cutting board, with the dark side down and the tail away from you.

🔺 Steady the fish with your guide hand. Make a cut at the tail straight down to the bone.

🔺 Using the tip of your knife, make a shallow incision all the way around the perimeter of the fish, just above the fins.

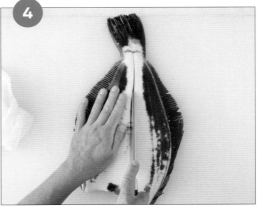

🔺 Locate the lateral line of the fish (see page 57). Steadying the fish with your guide hand and with your index finger on the spine of the knife, cut along this line from the tail to the head, using the tip of your blade. Repeat until the knife has cut down to the spine.

▲ Returning to the top of the incision, insert the tip of the knife to the left of the spine, flush against the bones.

▲ Using your guide hand, lift the corner of the fillet and, with long sweeping strokes toward the head, cut the fillet away from the bones. (If you are left-handed, start on the fillet to the right of the spine.)

▲ Turn the fish so that the tail is facing you and the remaining fillet is now on your left. (If you are left-handed, it will be on your right.)

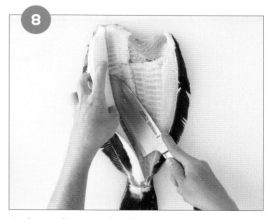

▲ Repeat Steps 5 and 6, this time working from the head toward the tail.

▲ Flip over the fish so the dark side is up and the tail is away from you.

▲ Repeat Steps 2 to 8 to remove the two remaining fillets.

Western-Style Filleting

Western-style filleting is similar to the *daimyo oroshi* method used in Japan, which is considered wasteful because it leaves more meat on the bone than the *sanmai oroshi* technique. Before filleting in either style, complete *mizuarai* (scaling and cleaning the fish; see page 58). Filleting can be done with or without the head on the fish. If you want to remove the head, follow the instructions on page 62.

EQUIPMENT

- *Deba*, chef's knife or filleting knife

TIP

When working with fish, you may want to use a small towel to protect your guide hand from the gills.

▲ Lay the cleaned fish on the cutting board, with the back facing you and the head facing your knife hand.

Although Western and Eastern filleting methods are different, both can successfully be accomplished using either a deba or a filleting knife. A chef's knife will also work for Western-style filleting.

▲ Use your guide hand to steady the fish. If you've cut off the head, skip to Step 5. If the head is still attached, place the knife blade under the pectoral fin, with the heel of the knife near the rear top of the skull.

▲ Holding the knife at a slight angle, cut down toward the head until you reach the spine.

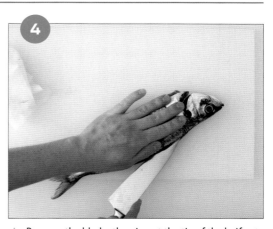

▲ Remove the blade; then insert the tip of the knife at the bottom of the incision you've just made, parallel to the board. Rest your guide hand on the side of the fish.

▲ Cut down the length of the fish, following a straight line just above the dorsal fin, until you reach the tail.

▲ When you reach the tail, push the knife through the belly, then out toward the tail to remove the tail section.

▲ Starting back at the head, repeat this cutting motion up to and along the spine, using your guide hand to lift the fillet as you cut. Remove the first fillet.

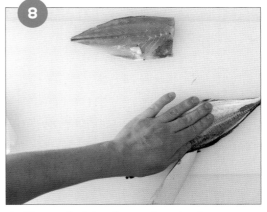

▲ Flip over the fish and repeat Steps 4 to 7 to remove the second fillet.

Preparing Shrimp for Tempura

In order to use shrimp tempura in *maki* (see page 229), the shrimp needs to be straightened to make rolling it into sushi possible. To achieve this, you will need to peel, devein, score and flatten the shrimp. Most shrimp are sold without the head. If your shrimp still has the head intact, pull it off before you begin.

EQUIPMENT

- *Deba*, paring or petty knife or chef's knife

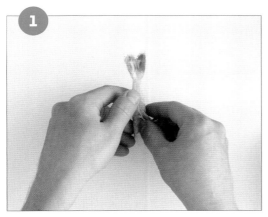

▲ Using your knife hand and starting at the tail end, drag your thumb down the length of the shrimp's belly to remove the legs.

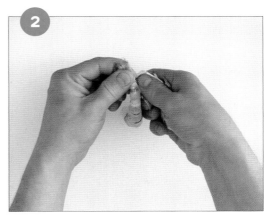

▲ Holding the shrimp by the tail with your guide hand, peel off the shell in one piece, leaving the tail in place.

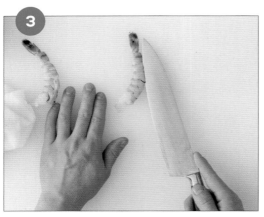

▲ Lay the shrimp on the cutting board with the back facing your knife hand.

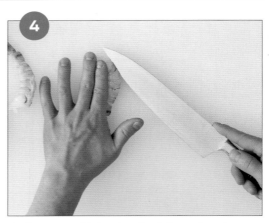

▲ Rest your guide hand on the shrimp to keep it steady. Holding the knife blade parallel to the board, place the tip of the knife at the head end of the shrimp.

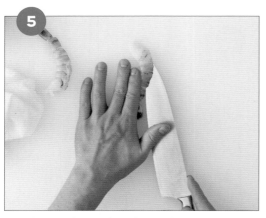

▲ Following the arc of the shrimp's back, gently roll the knife from its tip to its heel, making a shallow incision from head to tail just deep enough to reveal the intestine.

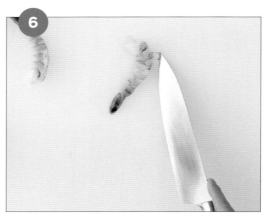

▲ Slide the tip of the knife underneath the intestine and then lift the intestine and pull it away.

▲ Rinse the shrimp under cool running water (see Tip, right) to remove any remaining waste.

TIP

Instead of using running water, some chefs rinse cleaned seafood in a basin of salted water (2 tbsp/30 mL salt per 4 cups/1 L water) to replicate seawater. This helps to maintain the natural flavor of the seafood.

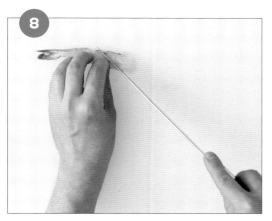

▲ With your guide hand, hold the peeled and deveined shrimp on the cutting board with the tail and belly facing up.

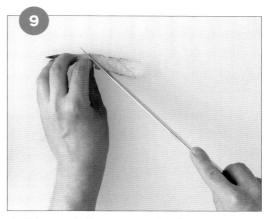

▲ Using your knife, score several shallow cuts crosswise along the length of the belly, being careful not to slice all the way through.

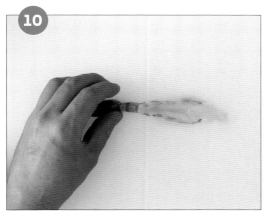

▲ Using your guide hand, hold the shrimp belly down on the cutting board.

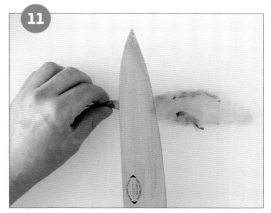

▲ Using the side of a chef's knife or *deba*, smack the shrimp on the back two or three times to flatten it. It is now ready to tempura.

Preparing Shrimp for *Nigiri*

When shrimp are prepared for *nigiri*, they are cooked first and then peeled and deveined. Before cooking, a bamboo skewer is carefully inserted under the shrimp's shell to straighten it. Once the skewer has been removed after cooking, you will be able to rest the shrimp flat on the rice.

EQUIPMENT

- Paring or petty knife
- Bamboo skewers
- Ice bath

TIP

Trimming the tail of the shrimp (Step 13) makes for a much prettier presentation (see page 228).

▲ *Cooking:* Fill a saucepan with water and bring to a boil. Fill a bowl halfway with ice and top up with cold water.

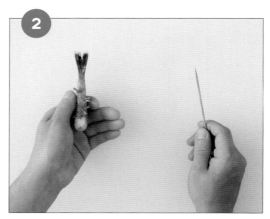

▲ Meanwhile, using your fingertips, hold the shrimp in your guide hand with the tail facing away from you and legs facing up.

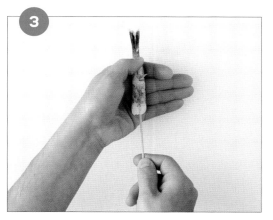

▲ Slowly insert a skewer beneath the shell on the belly side, being careful not to pierce the flesh. Set aside. Repeat with remaining shrimp.

▲ Place prepared shrimp in the boiling water and boil for 2 to 3 minutes, until shrimp is pink.

▲ Using a slotted spoon, transfer cooked shrimp to prepared ice bath and let sit until cool enough to handle.

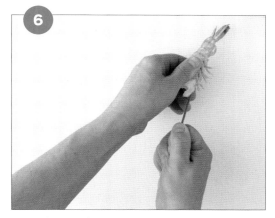

▲ *Peeling:* Carefully remove skewers from cooked shrimp.

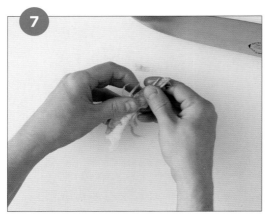

▲ Hold the shrimp with the tail and legs facing up. Drag your thumb down the length of the belly from tail to head to remove the legs.

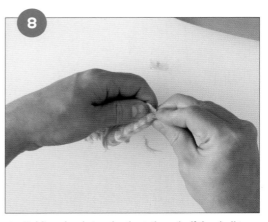

▲ Holding the shrimp by the tail, peel off the shell in one piece, leaving the tail in place.

▲ *Deveining and preparing:* Lay shrimp on cutting board with the belly up and tail facing away from you. Using your guide hand, pinch shrimp by the head end to hold it.

▲ Using the tip of the knife, cut down from head to tail through the flesh to the intestine, being careful not to pierce it.

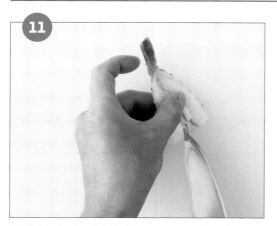

▲ Using the tip of the knife, scrape away intestine to remove it.

▲ Flip over shrimp and place on cutting board so back is up and tail is facing your knife hand.

▲ Trim off the end of the tail so that it has a flat, even appearance (you may want to steady the shrimp with your guide hand while doing this).

▲ Open up the shrimp like a book and lay it flat, cut side down, on the cutting board. The shrimp is now butterflied and ready to use.

Opening Clams

Clams (*aoyagi*) have two uses in sushi: the foot is used for *nigiri*, and the abductor muscle is used for *gunkanmaki* (you need to open a few clams to get enough abductor muscles for one *gunkanmaki*). The foot tastes like the ocean, while the muscle is slightly sweet.

EQUIPMENT

- Clam knife
- Kitchen towel or mesh glove

Clams and scallops are opened in a similar manner—from the front. The chief difference is in the tools you use to open them: scallop knives are shorter than clam knives, so there is less risk of cutting into the muscle.

▲ Grip the clam in your protected guide hand, with the hinge facing your hand.

▲ Place the knife blade with its sharp edge along the seam between the upper and lower shells.

▲ Using small sawing movements, slowly work the knife in between the top and bottom shells.

▲ Once the knife is partly inserted, twist it up toward you to pry the shells apart.

▲ Remove the knife and then reinsert it, point first, at the hinge end of the shell, keeping the blade flush with the very top of the shell.

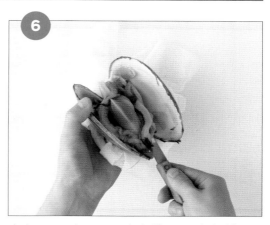

▲ In one motion, scrape the knife across the inside of the top shell to sever the muscle from the shell.

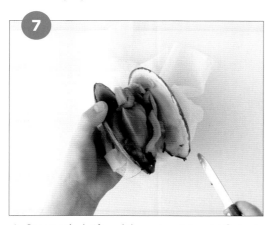

▲ Remove the knife and then reinsert it, point first, at the hinge end of the shell, keeping the blade flush with the very bottom of the shell.

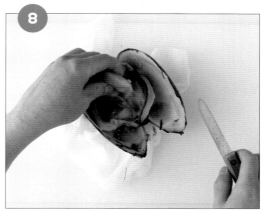

▲ In one motion, scrape the knife across the inside of the bottom shell to sever the muscle from the shell.

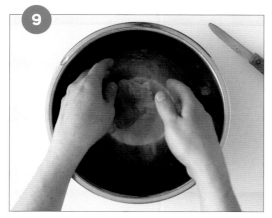

▲ Remove the clam and rinse under room-temperature running water. It is now ready to use.

TIPS

Clam knives are sharpened on one side so they can be forced between the shells. Always protect your guide hand when opening bivalves, either by holding the clam in a towel or by wearing a mesh glove (see page 95).

Always check your clams for life before opening (see page 56) and discard any dead ones. If you notice a foul smell when you open a clam, it's safest to dispose of it.

Preparing Scallops

Scallops (*hotate*) have a sweet, mild flavor and soft texture that make them excellent for *nigiri*. Scallops use a very large abductor muscle to open and close their shells rapidly, creating propulsion that enables them to move around the ocean floor—this muscle is the part of the scallop that we eat.

EQUIPMENT

- Scallop knife or filleting knife
- Tablespoon, optional
- Kitchen towel

TIP

Scallop knives are shorter than clam knives to ensure that you don't accidentally cut the flesh.

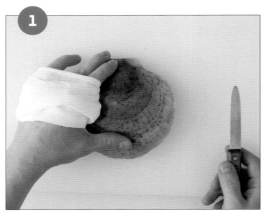

▲ With your guide hand wrapped in a small towel, place scallop on cutting board with bottom (concave side) facing down and front facing your knife hand.

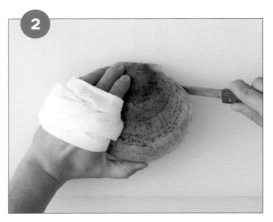

▲ Holding scallop steady with your guide hand, slide tip of knife between top and bottom shells, close to the hinge. Using a twisting motion, pry the shells open slightly.

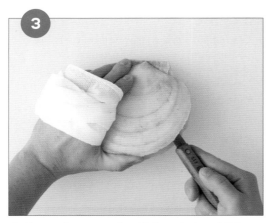

▲ Turn scallop over so flat side is on the board. Using your guide hand, steady scallop. Insert knife at far end.

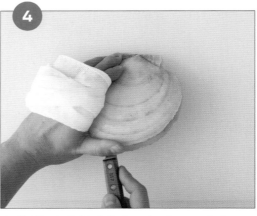

▲ Holding knife blade flush against bottom shell, scrape it across inside of shell to detach the muscle.

▲ Turn scallop over and, using your hands, open or remove top shell to expose the muscle.

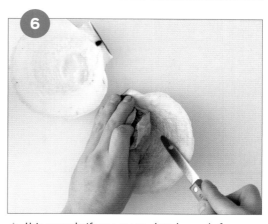

▲ Using your knife or a spoon, detach muscle from bottom shell.

▲ Using your fingers, pull away the frill and black stomach and discard. Pull away the orange roe (also called "coral") and reserve for another use.

▲ Pull away and discard the small, hard white muscle on the side of the larger abductor muscle.

▲ Rinse abductor muscle under cool running water or in a basin of salted water (2 tbsp/ 30 mL salt per 4 cups/ 1 L water). It is now ready to use.

TIPS

Scallop roe is not used in sushi but many people enjoy it. It needs to be cooked—light poaching works well.

To use scallops for *nigiri*, butterfly each scallop and place on rice. To butterfly a scallop, place it flat side down on the cutting board and hold it steady with your guide hand. Using a petty, paring or chef's knife, cut scallop in half horizontally, stopping just shy of severing it all the way through. Open it up like a book lying flat.

Preparing Soft-Shell Crab

Soft-shell crabs (*sofuto sheru kurabu*) are a seasonal delight available from May to July. They are used to make spider rolls, which are Western inside-out rolls (*uramaki*, see page 235).

EQUIPMENT

- Chef's knife
- Kitchen shears

Soft-shell crabs are blue crabs that have molted their shells, and they fatten up during molting and develop a rich flavor. Make sure the crabs are alive when you purchase them (a little movement is all you need to see).

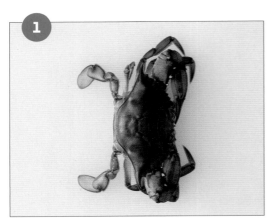

▲ Place live crab on cutting board, right side up, with head facing your knife hand.

▲ Hold crab steady with your guide hand. Using kitchen shears, cut off the face just behind the eyes (the crab will die instantly).

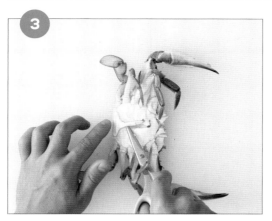

▲ Turn crab on its back and locate the apron (a flap at the rear of the crab).

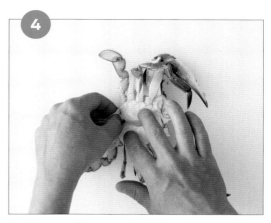

▲ Using your fingers, peel back the apron and pull it off, twisting as you pull.

▲ Flip crab over again. Lift one side of the top shell, or carapace, to expose the gills.

▲ Use your fingers to pull out the gills, or cut them out using your knife or shears.

▲ Repeat Steps 5 and 6 on other side of shell. Rinse under cool running water. The crab is now ready to tempura (see page 223).

Preparing King Crab Legs

King crabs (*tarabagani*) are prized for their meatiness and sweet flavor. Because the meat spoils so quickly, king crab legs are cooked and frozen on the boat, right after they have been caught in the cold waters of Alaska. To remove the meat, all you need is a good pair of kitchen shears.

EQUIPMENT

- Kitchen shears

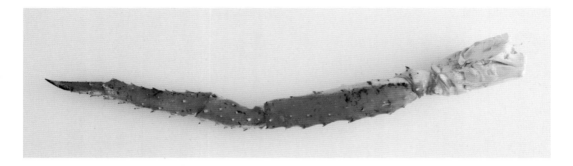

▲ Hold a crab leg in both hands, with one hand on either side of a joint. Bend the joint in its opposite direction to break it apart. Repeat with remaining joints.

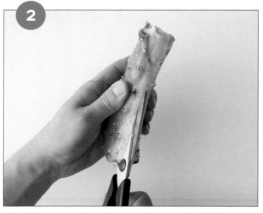

▲ Hold one section of leg in your guide hand. Using your other hand, open the scissors and slide the bottom blade into the end closest to you.

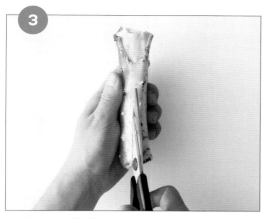

▲ Cut the shell of the leg piece from one end to the other.

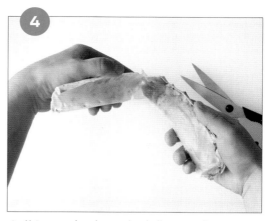

▲ Using your hands, pry the shell open and remove the meat.

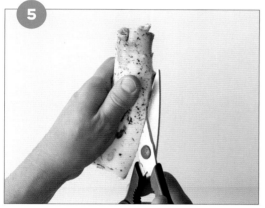

▲ If the shell is too difficult to open, rotate the leg 180 degrees and repeat Steps 2 to 4.

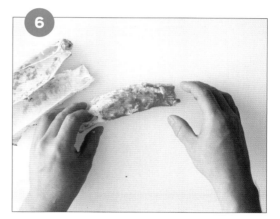

▲ Discard shells. Rinse crabmeat under cool running water and pat dry with paper towels. The meat is ready to use.

PREPARING SNOW CRAB LEGS

Snow crab legs look and taste similar to those of king crabs but are easier to open because their shells are more flexible. Simply grab a segment with both hands and, with your thumbs extended toward each other, bend until it breaks. Pull out the meat. If a segment gives you trouble, simply get out your kitchen shears and follow the steps for preparing king crabs.

Preparing Sea Urchin

In our opinion, sea urchin (*uni*) is one of the greatest delicacies in the world. Its taste is described as essence of the ocean. What you are eating is its orange roe. If you are not buying *uni* that has already been removed from the shell, purchase only fresh, live sea urchins (see page 56)—when frozen, *uni* becomes unpalatable.

EQUIPMENT

- Kitchen shears
- Teaspoon
- Small bowl filled with salted water (see Tips, right)
- Nonstick gloves, optional
- Gloves (see Tips, right)

TIPS

When handling sea urchins, wear gloves or wrap your guide hand in a small towel to protect yourself from being pricked.

To replicate seawater, in a bowl, combine 1 tbsp (15 mL) salt and 2 cups (500 mL) water. Dunking the roe in salted water helps to maintain the natural flavor of the *uni*.

1

▲ Place sea urchin upside down on board with beak facing up

2

▲ Open shears and insert bottom blade next to the beak. Make an incision ½ to ¾ inch (1 to 2 cm) long, depending on the size of the sea urchin.

▲ Using the length of the incision as your radius and the beak as the center, cut a circle around the beak.

▲ Remove the cut part to reveal the inside of the sea urchin. You will see black guts and orange tongues of roe—these "tongues" are the *uni*.

▲ Using a spoon, carefully remove the delicate sacs of roe.

▲ Dunk roe in salted water (see Tip, page 94) to rinse clean. The *uni* is now ready for use.

WORKING WITH GLOVES

Disposable nonstick gloves are useful in any kitchen, but are especially practical in sushi kitchens where you are working with sticky rice. Not only do they help to keep sushi rice from sticking to your hands, but they also allow you to work more cleanly. Gloves come in a variety of materials, including latex and—if you're allergic to latex—nitrile, vinyl and plastic. When shucking oysters, scallops and clams as well as handling sea urchin, you may want to wear gloves that offer a little more protection. In these cases, metal or Kevlar cut-resistant gloves are a good choice. Both nonstick and cut-resistant gloves can be found in well-stocked kitchen supply stores.

Preparing Squid

Squid (*ika*) is used in both sushi and sashimi. For sashimi, the squid mantle (body) is often prepared using the pinecone cut (*matsukasa-giri*, page 131) to enhance texture and appearance. Squid legs are not used in sushi, but you can save them for other uses (see Tip, below).

EQUIPMENT

• *Deba* or chef's knife

In Japan, calamari is called ika kara-age.

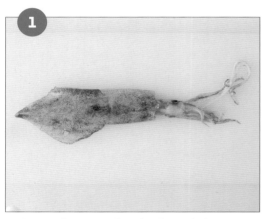

▲ Lay squid on cutting board with mantle facing your guide hand.

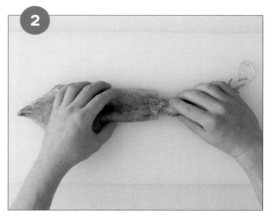

▲ Grasp the head and legs in your knife hand and the mantle in your guide hand. Gently pull the legs, head and organs away from the mantle (they should slip out easily). If you plan on using the legs, place your knife just behind the eyes and cut straight down; discard head and beak.

TIP

Save the squid legs after removing them. The legs can be blanched and placed on a sashimi plate. You can use them to make grilled calamari. They can also be used to add umami to your eel sauce during the reduction period.

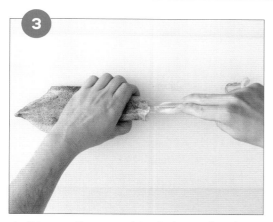

▲ Using your fingers, reach inside the mantle and pull out the thin, clear cartilage (sometimes called the "quill"); discard.

▲ Using your fingers, pull off and discard the fins on each side of the mantle.

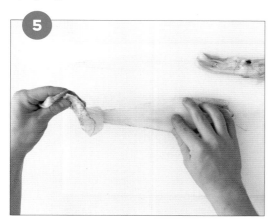

▲ Pull off the thin membrane covering the mantle; discard.

▲ Thoroughly rinse inside of mantle under cool running water, using your fingers to pull out any residual bits of organs. Pat dry with paper towels. The mantle is now ready to cut for *nigiri* or sashimi (see pages 127 to 137).

TIP

Squid ink (*ika-suma*) is a natural food coloring. It can be used in sauces, soups, pastas—virtually any food you want to turn black.

Sashimi

Sliced Raw Fish and Seafood (Sashimi)

SASHIMI IS THE PUREST way to eat fish. In most instances it is simply sliced raw fish or seafood, although sometimes it is cooked or lightly blanched to improve texture or add flavor. In Japan, sashimi made with horsemeat or chicken tenders is also popular. Even though sashimi is a staple of the sushi bar, it is technically not considered sushi, because it has no rice.

Because sashimi is served without rice or vinegar (which would mask the flavor of the fish), it is important to use the freshest fish available. This means choosing fish at the height of its season (using fish local to your area makes this easier).

Any fish that you would use to make sushi can also be used for sashimi. This includes tobiko and salmon roe as well as various types of tuna, snapper, salmon and squid, which are available year-round. In the winter months, it is best to look for wild yellowtail, mackerel and flounder. This is also the best season for sea urchin (*uni*). Spring is snapper season, and you will be able to find assorted species, from large to small, in an array of different colors. Spring also welcomes the first skipjack tuna (bonito) of the season. In the spring, bonito is firm and ruby red; it develops a nice fattiness into the fall. Summer is the best season for sea eel (*anago*) and freshwater eel (*unagi*), and on the east coast of North America, striped bass is also at its peak. From mid-May to September, look for wild (Pacific) salmon; in fall it is best to look for fresh sockeye salmon and salmon roe (*ikura*), as well as Atlantic tuna.

Knife Skills are Key

Sashimi shows off a chef's knife skills. Cutting sashimi is an art form that transforms fish into something beautiful and flavorful. Minute alterations in cutting technique can drastically alter the texture of a fish. The type of fish determines which cutting technique you'll use, but as a rule, the tougher the fish, the thinner the cut. Thin cuts range from the *sogizukuri* (page 119), at $1/8$ inch (3 mm), to the super-thin *usuzikuri* (page 123). If a fish is extremely tough, scoring the flesh by using the *yaezukuri* cut is the best way to improve mouthfeel (see page 107). For softer-fleshed fish, use the thickest cut, *hirazukuri* (page 103), which yields slices up to $1/2$ inch (1 cm) thick.

In order for the pure flavors of sashimi to be enjoyed, it is traditionally served at the beginning of a meal. Three to five slices are usually presented on individual shallow dishes or as part of a larger platter of fish and shellfish. The sashimi slices usually rest against a bed of shredded daikon, with shiso and wasabi alongside (see Garnishes for Sashimi, opposite). Stronger-flavored fish such as mackerel and seared fish may also be accompanied by grated ginger and finely sliced green onion. Some restaurants may serve sashimi with a thicker soy sauce that has been reduced with sake and bonito flakes. Depending on the fish used, sashimi may also be served with ponzu, a citrus- or vinegar-flavored soy sauce (see page 29).

To eat sashimi, first pour the soy sauce into a small dipping bowl. Using chopsticks, place a small dab of wasabi on the fish. Pick up the fish with your chopsticks and lightly dip it in the soy sauce. Place the whole piece in your mouth and enjoy the fresh, delicious flavor. For even more flavor, wrap the fish in shiso. You may also eat the shredded daikon as a palate cleanser between bites.

GARNISHES FOR SASHIMI (*TSUMA*)

Sashimi is usually served with a garnish. In Japanese these garnishes are referred to as *tsuma*. The most common is shredded daikon, which is placed under the sashimi to prop it up; the daikon can also be eaten as a palate cleanser after the sashimi has been consumed (see page 109 for information on preparing daikon garnish).

Shiso leaves are another common *tsuma*. These are usually placed between the daikon and the sliced fish. The shiso can be consumed with the fish (wrapped around the sashimi) or as a palate cleanser afterward.

Other *tsuma* include sliced citrus, grated peeled daikon or ginger, wasabi, wakame seaweed, shiso buds, diced ginger shallots (*myōga*) and sliced green onions.

Thick-Cut Sashimi *Hirazukuri*

Hirazukuri is the most versatile sashimi cut, as it can be applied to almost any type of soft-fleshed fish. It is also used for making *chirashi* (see page 163). The thick rectangular slices of fish produced by this technique can be anywhere from $\frac{1}{8}$ inch (3 mm) to $\frac{1}{2}$ inch (1 cm) thick, depending on your preference—$\frac{1}{4}$ inch (5 mm) is most common. It is demonstrated on page 104. As you practice, your cuts will improve. To ensure clean slices, be sure to wipe the knife blade occasionally with a damp towel (it may get a bit sticky, depending on the fish).

MAKES
4 SERVINGS
3 to 5 slices per serving

EQUIPMENT

- Cutting board
- Wet towel
- Nonstick gloves, optional
- *Yanagiba*, slicing knife or chef's knife
- Plating chopsticks (*moribashi*), optional

TIPS

Use this technique with any type of soft-fleshed fish, such as tuna, salmon, yellowtail or snapper.

For very soft-fleshed fish, you may cut thicker slices, up to $\frac{1}{2}$ inch (1 cm). The firmer the fish, the thinner you should cut it—as thin as $\frac{1}{8}$ inch (3 mm)—otherwise it will be chewy to eat.

If using a fillet, if one side is thicker, the thick side should be facing away from you.

If using tuna or salmon and the fillets are rectangular, cut against the grain of the fish.

1 lb	block or fillet of soft-fleshed fish (see Tips, left)	500 g
1 cup	shredded daikon (see page 109)	250 mL
4	shiso leaves	4
2 tbsp	wasabi paste	30 mL
	Soy sauce	

VARIATION

***Cube-Cut Sashimi* (Kaku-zukuri*):* The *kaku-zukuri* cut is good for thicker soft-fleshed fish, such as tuna, as well as for making *bara chirashi* (see page 171). The technique is the same as for the *hirazukuri* cut, but in Steps 2 and 3 you slice the fillet into $\frac{3}{4}$-inch (2 cm) strips. Then, instead of sliding the pieces of sashimi away from the fillet in Step 4, you leave them in place on the cutting board, rotate the fish 90 degrees, and cut straight down to make $\frac{3}{4}$-inch (2 cm) cubes. Serve as you would *hirazukuri*.

While you can eat sushi either with your fingers or chopsticks, etiquette demands that sashimi be eaten only with chopsticks.

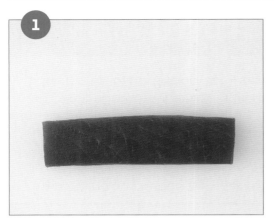

▲ Place block (or fillet) lengthwise on cutting board, skin side up and with tail end toward your guide hand and head end toward your cutting hand (see Tips, below).

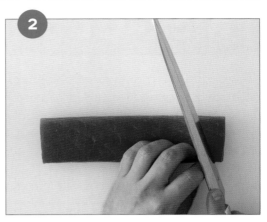

▲ Hold knife at a 45-degree angle, with tip up and index finger extended along spine of knife. Place heel of knife ¼ inch (0.5 cm) from head of fillet.

▲ Using a smooth rocking motion from heel to tip, cut through fillet, bringing tip of knife down on board as you slice.

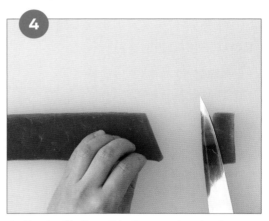

▲ Use tip of knife to slide slice away from head.

▲ Repeat Steps 2 to 4 until you have desired number of slices or entire fillet is cut.

TIPS

This cut was demonstrated using a block of tuna. If using fish with thinner fillets, such as snapper or yellowtail, when serving, place the thick side of the fillet facing away from you, skin side up.

If desired, add a slice of citrus, such as lemon, lime or yuzu, to brighten up the plate. See also Garnishes for Sashimi (page 101). you might also like to personalize the soy sauce you use (see page 16).

▲ To serve, place a mound of shredded daikon in center of serving plate. Beside daikon, place a shiso leaf. Arrange sashimi slices against daikon and shiso so daikon holds sashimi upright.

▲ Garnish each plate with a small dab of wasabi. Serve immediately with a small dipping bowl of soy sauce (see Tips, opposite).

PREPARING PERFECT SASHIMI

- Most Japanese supermarkets sell prepackaged fillets of sashimi fish. This is a great option, as it cuts down on your prep time and allows you to buy an assortment of types without having to buy whole fish.
- For best results, fillet and skin the fish just before cutting (see pages 64 to 71).
- Don't use pressure or force when cutting—let the knife do the work.
- When slicing sashimi, always pull the knife toward you through the fish, rather than pushing or sawing.
- Use the whole knife when slicing, not just the tip. This will give you more control and even, clean cuts.
- Be sure to wipe your knife clean between cuts, as needed.
- To keep freshness at its peak, fillet all fish in advance and skin the fish only when you are ready to prepare the sashimi. Prepare your garnishes in advance as well.

Double-Cut or Crosshatch Sashimi (*Yaezukuri*)

The *yaezukuri* cut is a variation on the thick cut (*hirazukuri*). It involves scoring the fish before cutting in the *hirazukuri* style. This method is used for silver-skinned fish such as mackerel (*saba, aji*), yellowtail (*hamachi*) and amberjack (*kanpachi*). It gives a better texture and flavor to the fish and also exposes the color of the meat for a more pleasing appearance. In addition, it allows the chef to show off his or her knife skills.

Once the scoring is done, you use the *hirazukuri* technique (see page 103) to cut the sashimi. Version 1 (pages 107 to 109) will yield a single slice of sashimi with a second line running end-to-end down the center. Version 2 (pages 111 to 113) will yield two rows of squares. Version 3 (pages 115 to 117) will yield diamonds instead of squares.

Double-Cut or Crosshatch Sashimi
Yaezukuri Version 1

This version of the *yaezukuri* cut yields a slice of sashimi ¼ inch (0.5 cm) thick with a scored line running from end to end down the center.

MAKES ABOUT 30 PIECES
(see Tip, page 108)

EQUIPMENT

- Cutting board
- *Yanagiba*, slicing knife or chef's knife
- Wet towel

TIPS

When slicing mackerel, you need to use an entire fillet, as mackerel oxidizes quickly.

Wipe your knife clean with the wet towel as needed.

1½ lbs	skinless silver-skinned fish, such as amberjack (*kampachi*), fillet	750 g
1 cup	shredded daikon, optional	250 mL
6	shiso leaves, optional	6
	Wasabi paste	
	Pickled ginger (*Gari*; page 27)	
	Soy sauce	

VARIATION

You can use this technique to slice mackerel and yellowtail as well as amberjack.

▲ Place fillet lengthwise on cutting board near the edge closest to you, skin side up and with tail end toward your guide hand and head end toward your cutting hand.

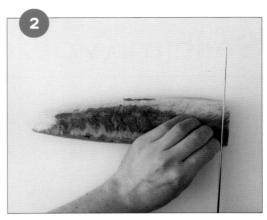

▲ Starting 1/8 inch (3 mm) from head end of fillet, make a score 1/8 inch (3 mm) deep, running lengthwise from one side of fillet to the other.

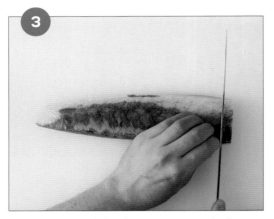

▲ Using your guide hand to measure, move knife 1/8 inch (3 mm) from the score toward tail. Holding knife at a 45-degree angle, with tip up and index finger extended along spine of knife, use a smooth rocking motion from heel to tip to cut through fillet, bringing tip down to the board as you slice. Use tip of knife to slide slice out of the way.

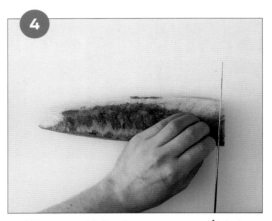

▲ Using your guide hand to measure, move 1/8 inch (3 mm) toward tail from the slice you have just made. Make a score 1/8 inch (3 mm) deep, running lengthwise from one side of fillet to the other.

TIPS

When preparing sashimi, work quickly—score, slice, score, slice—and repeat. Establishing a rhythm will make it easier.

Typically you would serve 2 to 3 pieces of sashimi per person. Cut and serve only as much sashimi as you will need at a time. Wrap remaining fish tightly in plastic wrap and refrigerate for up to 24 hours.

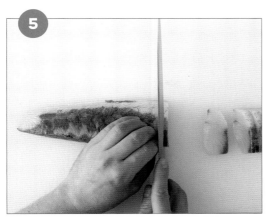

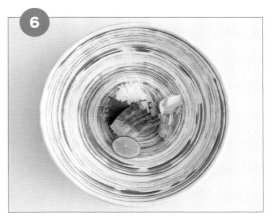

▲ Repeat Steps 3 and 4 until you have cut desired number of sashimi slices or entire fillet is sliced.

▲ To serve, if using, place a mound of shredded daikon in the center of each plate. Beside daikon, place a shiso leaf, if using. Arrange sashimi slices against daikon and shiso so daikon holds sashimi upright. Garnish with wasabi, ginger and a small dipping bowl of soy sauce.

ORDERING AT THE SUSHI BAR

The great thing about sitting at the sushi bar is that you can see all the amazing seafood displayed in front of you and order what appeals to you. If you don't feel like choosing, you can always ask the chef to pick for you—this is known as *omakase*, which translates as "in the chef's hands." Be sure to let the chef know your likes and dislikes as well as any allergies (to shellfish or gluten, for example). A typical meal starts with an assortment of sashimi, followed by *nigiri* sushi and ending with a *maki* roll or *temaki* hand roll. You usually finish with a piece of *tamago* or *kasutera* and tea.

DAIKON GARNISH FOR SASHIMI

Shredded daikon is a standard garnish for sashimi. It is cut in the *katsuramuki* style (see page 24) to create ribbons, then the ribbons are cut (julienned) into thin matchsticks.

For an added kick, use spicy daikon (*momiji oroshi*): grated daikon and red chile peppers. You can find it at Japanese markets or make it yourself. In a small bowl, combine 1½ to 2 tsp (7 to 10 mL) of your favorite dried chile powder (your choice depends on how much spice you like) and ¼ cup (60 mL) grated daikon.

Double-Cut or Crosshatch Sashimi
Yaezukuri Version 2

This version of the *yaezukuri* cut yields pieces of sashimi ½ inch (1 cm) thick with two rows of squares across the top. Only use this technique if you are planning to cut the entire fillet, as the scored fish will begin to discolor if left to sit for long. Version 1 of this cut (page 107) is the currently fashionable cut for silver-skinned fish, particularly in a busy restaurant setting, where speed is a must. This cut and Version 3 (page 115) are the more traditional presentations.

MAKES ABOUT 2 SERVINGS

2 to 3 slices
per serving

EQUIPMENT

- Cutting board
- *Yanagiba*, slicing knife or chef's knife
- Wet towel

TIP

When preparing sashimi, work quickly—score, slice, score, slice—and repeat. Establishing a rhythm will make it easier.

4 oz	skinless Boston mackerel (*saba*) fillet, or other skinless silver-skinned fish, such as amberjack (*kampachi*), yellowtail (*hamachi*) or *aji*, *shima aji* belly cuts	125 g
¼ cup	shredded daikon, optional	60 mL
2	shiso leaves, optional	2
	Wasabi paste	
	Pickled ginger (*Gari*; page 27)	
	Soy sauce	

When you first sit down at the sushi bar, you will be provided with a hot wet towel (oshibori) to clean your hands. If you plan on using your fingers to eat sushi, roll or fold up the oshibori the way it came and keep it to one side to clean your fingers between each piece. Some higher-end sushi bars provide a small folded wet cloth in what looks like a soy sauce dish to clean your fingers between sushi pieces.

▲ Place skinned fillet lengthwise on cutting board, with head end toward you and tail away from you.

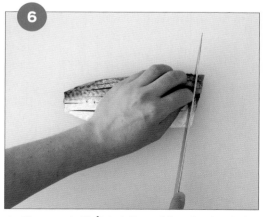

▲ Using your guide hand, measure $\frac{1}{4}$ inch (0.5 cm) from side of fillet closest to guide hand. Make a score $\frac{1}{8}$ inch (3 mm) deep down entire length of fillet.

▲ Move your guide hand $\frac{1}{4}$ inch (0.5 cm) from previous score and make another score $\frac{1}{8}$ inch (3 mm) deep down entire length of fillet.

▲ Repeat Step 3 until you have scored entire surface of fillet.

▲ Rotate fillet 90 degrees so tail is toward your guide hand.

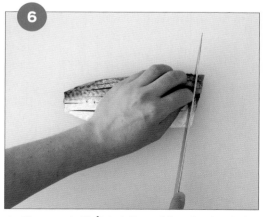

▲ Place your knife $\frac{1}{4}$ inch (0.5 cm) from head end of fillet and make a score $\frac{1}{8}$ inch (3 mm) deep, running from side to side.

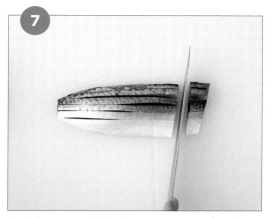

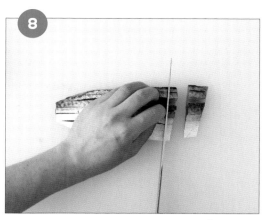

▲ Using your guide hand to measure, move ¼ inch (0.5 cm) from score toward tail end. Holding knife at a 45-degree angle with tip up and index finger extended along spine of knife, cut through fillet, using a smooth rocking motion from heel to tip to bring tip down to the board as you slice.

▲ Using your guide hand to measure, move ¼ inch (0.5 cm) toward tail end from slice you have just made. Make a score ⅛ inch (3 mm) deep across fillet from side to side.

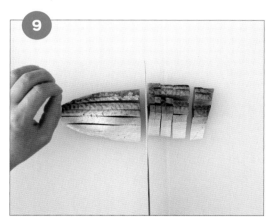

▲ Repeat Steps 7 and 8 until entire fillet is sliced.

▲ To serve, if using, place a mound of shredded daikon in center of serving plate. Beside daikon, place a shiso leaf, if using. Arrange sashimi slices against daikon and shiso so daikon holds sashimi upright. Serve immediately to avoid fish discoloring. Garnish with wasabi, ginger and a small dipping bowl of soy sauce.

TIPS

Between cuts, wipe your knife clean with the wet towel as needed.

To keep freshness at its peak, fillet the fish ahead of time but don't remove the skin until you are ready to prepare the sashimi.

Crosshatch-Cut Sashimi
Yaezukuri Version 3

This technique is similar to Version 2 of the double-cut or crosshatch sashimi cut (*yaezukuri*) except that it produces a diamond pattern instead of squares.

MAKES ABOUT 2 SERVINGS

2 to 3 slices per serving

EQUIPMENT

- Cutting board
- *Yanagiba*, slicing knife or chef's knife
- Wet towel

TIPS

For best results, fillet the fish just before cutting.

When preparing sashimi, work quickly—score, slice, score, slice—and repeat. Establishing a rhythm will make it easier.

4 oz	skinless Boston mackerel (*saba*) fillet, or other skinless silver-skinned fish, suh as amberjack (*kampachi*), yellowtail (*hamachi*), or *aji*, *shima aji* and salmon belly cuts	125 g
¼ cup	shredded daikon (see page 109), optional	60 mL
2	shiso leaves	2
	Wasabi paste	
	Pickled ginger (*Gari*; page 27)	
	Soy sauce	

When eating sashimi, add a small amount of wasabi directly to the fish and dip lightly into the soy. Sashimi is best enjoyed when it is eaten with the garnishes provided. You can wrap the fish with the shiso leaves provided or eat it with a little of the shredded daikon. Depending on the fish you can also add a bit of grated ginger, chopped scallions, or spicy daikon.

▲ Place fillet on cutting board at a 45-degree angle, with tail toward you and head end up and toward your cutting hand.

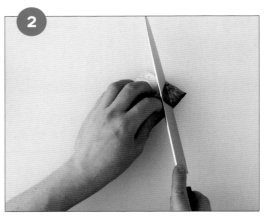

▲ Using your guide hand, measure $\frac{1}{4}$ inch (0.5 cm) from head end. Using the tip of your knife, make a score $\frac{1}{8}$ inch (3 mm) deep from one side of fillet to the other.

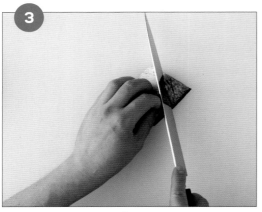

▲ Move your guide hand $\frac{1}{4}$ inch (0.5 cm) from previous score and make another score $\frac{1}{8}$ inch (3 mm) deep.

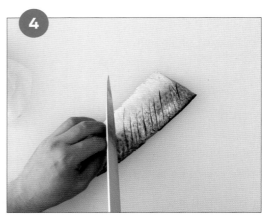

▲ Repeat Step 3 until you have scored fillet from head to tail.

▲ Rotate fillet so that it is at a 45-degree angle with head end toward your guide hand.

TIPS

To keep freshness at its peak, fillet the fish ahead of time but don't remove the skin until you are ready to prepare the sashimi.

Use the wet towel as needed to keep your knife clean.

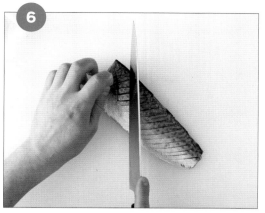

▲ Repeat Steps 2 and 3 to create a crosshatch pattern.

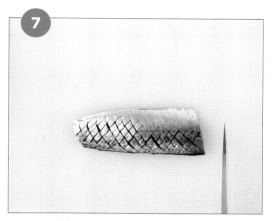

▲ Rotate fillet 90 degrees so that it is near the edge of cutting board, with tail end facing your guide hand.

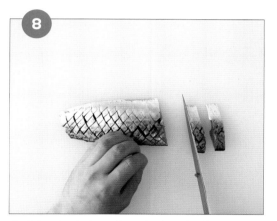

▲ Using the thick-cut (*hirazukuri*) method (see page 103), cut fillet into 1/2-inch (1 cm) pieces.

Remember to always use chopsticks when eating sashimi—never use your fingers, which is acceptable with sushi.

▲ To serve, if using, place a mound of shredded daikon in center of serving plate. Beside daikon, place a shiso leaf, if using. Arrange sashimi slices against daikon and shiso so daikon holds sashimi upright. Serve immediately to avoid fish discoloring. Garnish with wasabi, ginger and a small dipping bowl of soy sauce.

Thin-Cut Sashimi *Sogizukuri*

In contrast to the *hirazukuri* technique, which is executed with the knife straight up and down and produces thick slices of sashimi, this cut is done at a shallow angle (40 to 45 degrees) to produce thin slices (*sogizukuri*). The angle and thinness help to improve the texture of firmer, more fibrous fish such as sea bream and snapper. (It is also used to make *nigiri*). Typical *sogizukuri* slices are around ⅛ inch (3 mm) thick, depending on the fish and the texture you want to achieve. To make this cut, you must position your knife at a 40- to 45-degree angle toward the head of the fillet and start cutting from the tail end first.

MAKES 3 TO 5 SERVINGS

3 to 5 slices per serving

EQUIPMENT

- Cutting board
- Wet towel
- *Yanagiba,* slicing knife or chef's knife
- Plating chopsticks (*moribashi*), optional

12 oz	firm-fleshed fish, such as snapper fillet	375 g
	Shredded daikon (page 109)	
	Shiso leaves	
	Wasabi paste	
	Pickled ginger (*Gari*; page 27)	
	Soy sauce	

VARIATION

When making sushi, this traditional cut can be used on all fish.

TIPS

You can increase or decrease the thickness of the cut according to the toughness of the fish—the tougher the fish, the thinner the cut should be (and vice versa).

Step 4 creates a sharp edge, which looks more attractive on the plate.

Use the wet towel as needed to keep your knife clean.

Serve about 3 slices of one type of fish per person.

If you are not using the entire fillet, wrap it in several layers of paper towel (to absorb moisture) and then in plastic wrap. Refrigerate.

Sogizukuri is the cut that you will use most often—not only is it used to prepare sashimi, it is also used to prepare nigiri toppings (such as tuna, salmon, yellowtail or white fish). When preparing sashimi, this cut is intended for use on firm-fleshed, tougher fish such as snapper or sea bream.

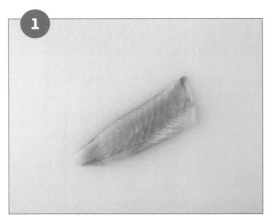

▲ Place fillet lengthwise on cutting board with tail toward your guide hand and head end toward your cutting hand, angling tail slightly toward edge of board.

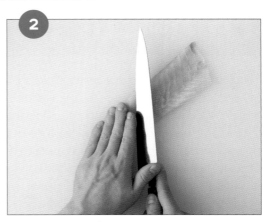

▲ With heel of knife positioned almost at the end of fillet's tail, angle spine of knife 45 degrees toward the head.

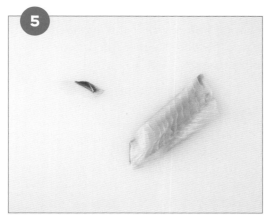

▲ Place the fingers of your guide hand on the area you are about to cut, in front of the blade. Pull knife toward you, slicing the fish, but not all the way through.

▲ When you get close to the tip of the knife, turn the blade to vertical and cut straight down.

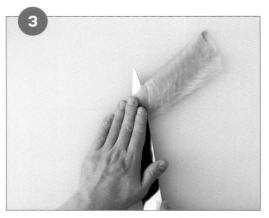

▲ Place cut piece at top of board.

▲ As you work, lay each cut at top of board, slightly overlapping the previous one.

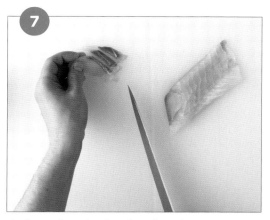

▲ Repeat Steps 2 to 5 until you have the amount you need or entire fillet is sliced.

▲ To serve, using your hands or *moribashi*, fold slices and stack on top of one another on a serving plate, or roll slices and arrange in a flower shape. Garnish with daikon, wasabi and a small dipping bowl of soy sauce.

SERVING PERFECT SASHIMI

- Sashimi should be served cold. To serve, fill a bowl with ice cubes or, preferably, crushed ice and top with bamboo leaves. Rest the sliced fish on the bamboo leaves. This makes for a great presentation and also keeps the fish cold but out of direct contact with the ice, which would make it watery. You can also refrigerate your serving plate or place it in the freezer for a few minutes to cool before serving. Never serve sashimi on a warm plate; this will draw out oils from the fish and create an unpleasant texture.

- Serve white fish and clams with salt and lemon sprinkled over them instead of soy sauce.

- For fattier fish, dab on a bit more wasabi before eating, to balance out the flavor (this goes for *nigiri* as well).

- For people who may be afraid to eat raw fish, you can sear or grill or use a torch to lightly cook tuna and salmon. You want to cook just the skin or outermost layer; the fish itself should remain raw.

Paper-Thin Sashimi
Usuzukuri

This cut is most often used with firm-fleshed white fish such as fluke, sea bass, snapper or blowfish (*fugu*). It is similar to *sogizukuri* (page 119), except that you cut each slice as thinly as possible and immediately transfer it to a serving plate. The translucent paper-thin slices are layered in a circular pattern to resemble a flower.

MAKES 1 PLATE SASHIMI

EQUIPMENT

- Cutting board
- Wet towel
- *Yanagiba*, slicing knife or chef's knife
- Plating chopsticks (*moribashi*), optional

TIPS

Chill serving plate before slicing fish.

Transfer each slice directly to serving plate after cutting. Because the slices are so thin, they will be difficult to handle if stacked on the cutting board.

Very fresh fish may be difficult to slice. If that is the case, set it aside at room temperature to warm up slightly, or refrigerate and use the following day.

Use the thinnest knife possible for this cut. A *fugubiki* knife, which is super-thin, is best, if you have one.

12 oz	firm white fish (fluke, sea bass or snapper) fillet	375 g
1 tbsp	finely sliced green onion	15 mL
1	slice citrus (*sudachi*, yuzu, lime or lemon)	1
2	shiso leaves, julienned	2
1 tbsp	spicy daikon (*momiji oroshi*, see page 109)	15 mL
	Ponzu sauce (see page 29)	

VARIATION

This technique may also be used for yellowtail (*himachi*). Serve with thinly sliced jalapeño, ponzu sauce and cilantro.

If ordering at a sushi bar, a general guideline is to start with the more delicate white fish before moving on to the richer, bolder flavors of tuna and yellowtail and then stronger-flavored fish such as mackerel. From there you can venture into savory seafoods such as marinated clams, ikura or eel and sweet tamago.

It is common to finish a sushi meal with rolled sushi, but in this day and age you should feel free to order it at any time.

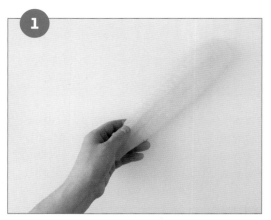

▲ Place fish lengthwise on cutting board with tail end toward your guide hand and head toward your cutting hand, angling tail end slightly toward edge of board.

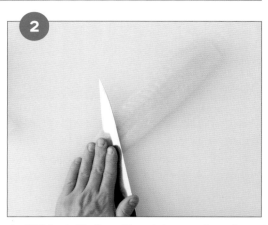

▲ With heel of knife positioned almost at the end of fillet's tail, angle spine of knife 45 degrees toward the head.

▲ Place the fingers of your guide hand on the area you are about to cut, in front of the blade. Pull knife toward you, slicing the fish but not all the way through.

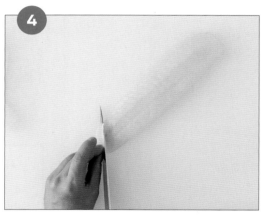

▲ When you get close to tip of knife, turn blade to vertical and cut straight down.

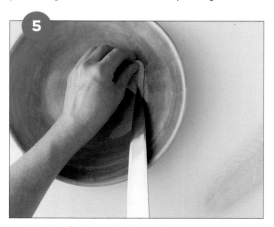

▲ Using knife, immediately transfer slice to a serving plate (see Tips, right). Place far end of slice near rim of plate and position near end toward center.

TIPS

To transfer fish to the plate, use the thumbs and forefinger of your guide hand to lift the far end of the slice and use the tip of the knife to support the near end of the slice.

After transferring each slice to the serving plate, use the heel of your guide hand to rotate the plate clockwise, making it easier to place the next slice.

Use the damp towel to wipe the knife as needed, to keep the fish from sticking or folding and to make it easier to slice.

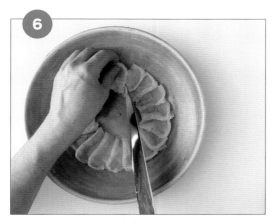

▲ Repeat Steps 2 to 5, slightly overlapping slices around circumference of plate, until plate is covered or whole fillet is sliced (see Tips, opposite).

▲ Place shiso leaf in the center of the plate. Arrange spicy daikon and green onions on shiso. Lean citrus slice against daikon and onion. Serve with a small dipping bowl of ponzu sauce (see page 29).

PUFFER FISH

In Japan, this slicing technique, using a *fugubiki* knife instead of a *yanagiba*, is the only way to prepare the deadly puffer fish (*fugu*). It is illegal to serve *fugu* in most countries outside of Japan—if sliced improperly it can kill the diner. In Japan, a chef must train for many years to learn how to slice *fugu* before he or she is legally allowed to serve it to guests.

Squid Cuts for Sashimi

Once you have cleaned your squid (see page 96), you can choose from several different cutting techniques to help tenderize it and create appealing texture.

These include the spotted-fawn cut (*kanoko-giri*), the pinecone cut (*matsukasa-giri*) and the spiral cut (*naruto-giri*). Each cut is explained in detail from pages 127 to 137.

Spotted-Fawn Cut
Kanoko-giri

In this technique, the scoring on the squid resembles the markings on the back of a young deer. It serves the double purpose of tenderizing the squid and making it look more appealing.

MAKES 4 TO 6 SERVING

3 pieces per serving

EQUIPMENT

- Cutting board
- *Yanagiba*, slicing knife or chef's knife

TIPS

Quickly blanching and shocking the squid after slicing helps to open up the cuts to show off your knife skills.

Instead of blanching the squid to open up and show off the cuts, you can simply butt the ends together, but the results won't be as dramatic.

1	squid, cleaned (see page 96) and sliced open lengthwise	1
2 tsp	wakame, rehydrated, optional (see Tips, page 129)	10 mL
	Wasabi paste	
	Pickled ginger (*Gari*; page 27)	
	Soy sauce	

VARIATION

Spotted-fawn-cut squid (*kanoko-giri*) can be placed on rice balls and served as *nigiri*.

The spotted-fawn cut and the pinecone cut are almost identical. The chief difference is a slight flaring of the scores in the pinecone cut, which are enhanced by blanching.

▲ Bring a large saucepan filled with water to a boil. Prepare an ice bath by filling a large bowl half full of ice and covering with water (see Tips, page 127).

▲ Lay cut squid flat on cutting board at a 45-degree angle, with wider end toward you and edge of cutting board, and pointed end toward your cutting hand.

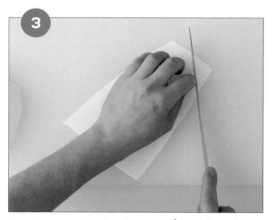

▲ Using your guide hand, measure $\frac{1}{8}$ inch (3 mm) from pointed end. Using tip of knife, make a shallow score from one side of squid to the other (see Tips, page 129).

▲ Move your guide hand $\frac{1}{8}$ inch (3 mm) from previous score and make another shallow cut. Repeat until entire surface of squid is scored.

▲ Rotate squid so top is angled toward your guide hand.

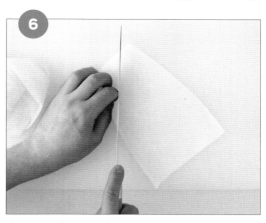

▲ Repeat Steps 3 and 4.

▲ Using tongs, a slotted spoon or a spider, very quickly dip prepared squid into boiling water and then transfer to prepared ice bath. Once cooled, remove from ice bath and pat dry with a paper towel.

▲ If using, place rehydrated wakame on serving plate. Cut squid into pieces (2- by 1-inch/5 by 2½ cm). Transfer to prepared plate. Garnish with wasabi, ginger and a small dipping bowl of soy sauce.

TIPS

If you prefer, you can square off the edges of the squid before scoring, for a neater presentation.

Make your scores shallow—no more than halfway through the flesh of the squid.

To rehydrate wakame, place in a small bowl and cover with water. Set aside for 30 minutes, until softened. Using your hands, squeeze out excess water.

Pinecone Cut *Matsukasa-giri*

This cut is almost identical to the spotted-fawn cut, except that instead of scoring straight up and down, you hold the knife at a 45-degree angle when cutting.

MAKES 4 TO 6 SERVING

3 pieces per serving

EQUIPMENT

- Cutting board
- *Yanagiba*, slicing knife or chef's knife

TIPS

Quickly blanching and shocking the squid after slicing helps to open up the cuts and show off your knife skills.

Instead of blanching the squid to open up and show off the cuts, you can simply butt the ends together, but the results won't be as dramatic.

1	squid, cleaned (see page 96) and sliced open lengthwise	1
3	shiso leaves	3
1	slice lemon, halved	1
	Sea salt	
	Wasabi paste	
	Soy sauce	

VARIATION

Squid cut with the pinecone cut (*matsukasa-giri*) can be placed on rice balls and served as *nigiri*.

The lattice-like patterns of this cut and the spotted-fawn cut do more than change the texture. They also help sauces adhere to the squid. Without the cuts, they would slide off the slippery surface.

▲ Bring a large saucepan filled with water to a boil. Prepare an ice bath by filling a large bowl half full of ice and covering it with water.

▲ Lay cut squid flat on cutting board at a 45-degree angle, with wider end toward you and edge of cutting board, and pointed end toward your cutting hand.

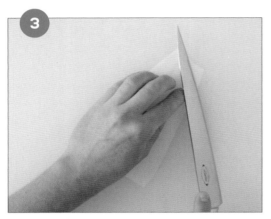

▲ Measure ⅛ inch (3 mm) from pointed end. Holding tip of knife at a 45-degree angle, make a shallow score from one side of squid to the other (see Tips, opposite).

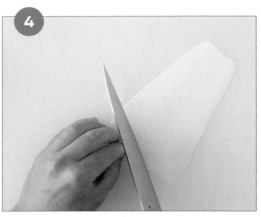

▲ Move your guide hand ⅛ inch (3 mm) from previous score and make another shallow score at a 45-degree angle. Repeat until entire surface of squid is scored.

TIPS

If you prefer, you can square off the edges of the squid before scoring, for a neater presentation.

Make your scores shallow—no more than halfway through the flesh of the squid.

▲ Rotate squid so top is angled toward your guide hand.

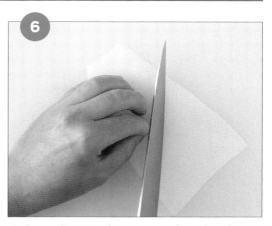

▲ Repeat Steps 3 and 4, starting at the wide end.

▲ Using tongs, a slotted spoon or a spider, very quickly dip prepared squid into boiling water and then transfer to prepared ice bath.

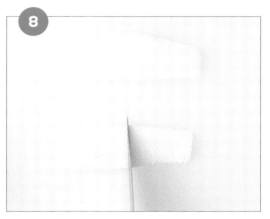

▲ Once cooled, remove from ice bath and pat dry with paper towel. Cut into rectangular pieces (2- by 1-inch/ 5 by 2½ cm).

▲ Roll squid (cut side up) and arrange on top of shiso leaves. Garnish with sliced lemon and a pinch of sea salt. Serve with wasabi and a small dipping bowl of soy sauce.

Spiral Cut *Naruto-giri*

This is a very attractive cut, and the shiso makes a nice contrast with the white flesh of the squid.

MAKES 1 SERVING

EQUIPMENT

- Cutting board
- *Yanagiba*, slicing knife or chef's knife

TIPS

If you prefer, you can square off the edges of the squid before scoring, for a neater presentation.

Make your scores shallow—no more than halfway through the flesh of the squid.

No blanching is necessary for this cut, as the rolling helps to open up the scores.

1	squid, cleaned (see page 96) and sliced open lengthwise	1
4 to 5	shiso leaves (enough to cover squid)	4 to 5
	Bamboo leaf (*sasa*), optional	
	Wasabi paste	
	Pickled ginger (*Gari*; page 27)	
	Soy sauce	

VARIATIONS

For a different flavor, substitute a small sheet of nori (cut to the size of your squared squid) for the shiso leaves.

Sprinkle with sesame and serve with grated ginger and ponzu.

Another "raw" preparation of squid is shiokara: Squid with its innards intact is sliced up and packed with salt then left to ferment for up to a month. The resulting fermented squid is eaten on its own with sake or beer or as an accompaniment to rice.

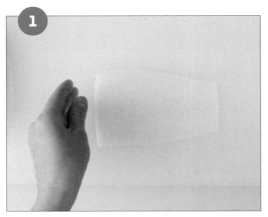

▲ Lay cut squid flat on cutting board, skin side down, with pointed end toward your guide hand.

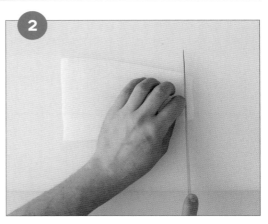

▲ Using your knife, trim off pointed end to create a square piece.

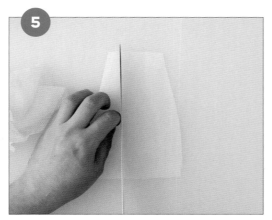

▲ Rotate squid so trimmed end is positioned at top.

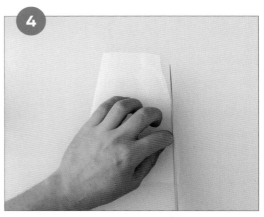

▲ Using your guide hand, measure $\frac{1}{8}$ inch (3 mm) from the side. Using tip of knife, make a shallow score from one end of squid to the other (see Tips, page 135).

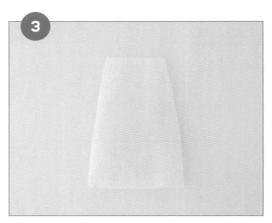

▲ Move your guide hand $\frac{1}{8}$ inch (3 mm) from previous score and make another shallow score. Repeat until entire surface of squid is scored.

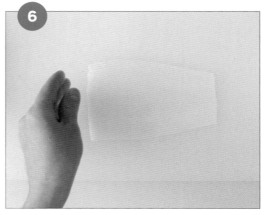

▲ Rotate squid so scores run parallel to edge of board closest to you. Flip squid over so cut side is facing down.

▲ Cover scored squid with shiso leaves, trimming any pieces that hang over edges.

▲ Starting at the bottom edge, roll squid into a cylinder. Place seam side down on board.

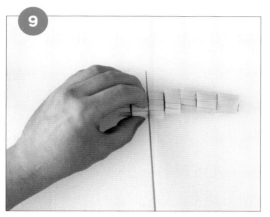

▲ Slice rolled squid into desired number of pieces.

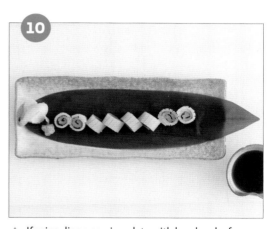

▲ If using, line a serving plate with bamboo leaf. Transfer prepared squid to serving plate. Garnish with wasabi, ginger and a small dipping bowl of soy sauce.

TIPS

Remember that sashimi should be served cold. Refrigerate your serving plate for a few minutes before serving. You might like to personalize the soy sauce you use (see page 16).

Sushi

Sushi Rice

RICE IS THE MOST important crop in Japan. It is eaten as part of every meal, and each Japanese citizen consumes about 132 pounds (60 kg) of rice per year. The Japanese word for cooked rice is *gohan*, which also means "meal." Rice originally made its way from China, through Korea, to Japan about 2,500 years ago. The growing and processing of rice, which was highly labor-intensive and required whole villages to cooperate at harvest-time, is believed to have contributed to Japan's communal culture.

Sushi rice (*shari*) is a combination of cooked Japonica rice, vinegar, sugar, salt and, if desired, *konbu*. Every sushi bar has its own well-guarded recipes for *shari*. Some use red rice wine vinegar for added punch, more sugar for sweetness, or more salt to suit their taste.

Cooking rice for sushi is different from cooking rice for any other purpose. You must use Japonica rice, which is a medium-grain rice about $2\frac{1}{2}$ times longer than it is wide—there is no substitute. It is grown in the United States as well as in Japan and is often sold in packages labeled "sushi rice." When it is prepared correctly, this variety has the appropriate amount of stickiness to make *nigiri* and sushi rolls or to be picked up and eaten with chopsticks. Shorter-grain rice will be too sticky, and longer grains will not be sticky enough. Cooked Japonica rice should be firm but tender, never mushy.

MAKING PERFECT SUSHI RICE

- Thoroughly rinsing the rice removes excess starch. This is important because it helps to ensure that the finished rice is sticky, but not too sticky. It also polishes the rice, which encourages vinegar absorption. Work quickly to ensure that the rice doesn't absorb too much water. Drain well after rinsing (see Steps 1 and 2, page 144).

- After adding the rice and water to the saucepan, you may allow it to soak for 30 minutes. Some chefs feel that a soaking period improves texture. If you prefer, use a rice cooker to cook your rice (see page 53). Some cookers include a soaking period.

- Never lift the lid while your rice is cooking. This will release precious steam, reducing the amount of cooking liquid available.

- The rice must be hot to absorb the vinegar, but it is then important to fan the rice to cool it and remove moisture. If you don't have a fan, use a blow-dryer on the coolest setting or a folded magazine.

- Before using it, sushi rice should be at room temperature—neither hot nor cold.

Another major difference when making sushi rice is the ratio of water to rice when cooking. While most rice applications use 2 to 3 parts water to 1 part rice, sushi rice is close to a 1:1 ratio. We say "close" because, depending on whether the rice is old crop or new crop, you will need to adjust the amount of water slightly (see Cooking New-Crop Rice versus Old-Crop Rice, right). If this still seems like very little water, remember that you will be adding liquid in the form of sushi vinegar after the rice is cooked.

Prepare your rice at least 2 hours and up to 6 hours in advance of when you plan to use it, so that it has time to cool to room temperature before assembling the sushi.

Cooking New-Crop Rice versus Old-Crop Rice

"New-crop" rice is the rice of that year's harvest and becomes available in the late fall; it is usually labeled as such on the package (although once January rolls around, this rice becomes "old crop"; see page 14). New-crop rice retains more moisture and so requires less water when cooking; follow the 1:1 water-to-rice ratio. "Old-crop" rice is drier and may require up to 1.25 parts water to 1 part rice when cooking. As old-crop rice gets older, it may require slightly more water. These ratios are guidelines only; you might have to experiment to find the ratio of water to rice that works best for your rice.

Sushi Vinegar *Awasezu*

Sushi vinegar needs to be made at least an hour before using so that it has time to cool before stirring into the rice.

MAKES ABOUT 1 CUP (250 ML)

EQUIPMENT

- Small saucepan

TIPS

This makes enough for 2 batches of Sushi Rice (page 143).

You may use red or white rice vinegar or equal parts of each. We like to use half of each for stronger acidity.

These quantities are a guideline. The sugar and salt can be adjusted up or down depending on your taste.

7 tbsp	red or white rice vinegar (see Tips, left)	105 mL
5 tbsp	granulated sugar	75 mL
2 tbsp	salt	30 mL
1	piece (4 inches/10 cm) *konbu*	1

1. In saucepan over medium heat, heat vinegar.
2. Add sugar and salt and bring to a simmer, stirring frequently until completely dissolved.
3. Remove from heat, add *konbu* and set aside for at least 1 hour to cool. If not using immediately, transfer to a resealable glass container and refrigerate for up to 1 year.

Before there was refrigeration, vinegar was used to kill bacteria and preserve rice and fish.

Sushi Rice *Shari*

Making rice for sushi is the most important thing you will learn in this book. Without good sushi rice, you can't make sushi. Apprentice chefs in Japan may take one to two years to perfect rice before they move on to fish. Using a rice cooker will take some of the guesswork out of cooking rice, but following this recipe will help you to cook it on the stovetop.

MAKES
4 CUPS (1 L)

EQUIPMENT

- Fine-mesh sieve
- Large bowl
- Heavy saucepan with tight-fitting lid
- *Hangiri*, optional (see Tips, below)
- Rice paddle (*shamoji*) or spatula
- Fan, optional (see Making Perfect Sushi Rice, page 140)

TIPS

While your rice is cooking, soak your *hangiri* and rice paddle in cold water to prevent sticking. Drain and wipe dry before adding the rice. If you don't have a *hangiri*, use a wide, shallow non-reactive bowl or a clean wooden salad bowl.

If you don't have a Japanese rice paddle (*shamoji*), use a wooden or silicone spatula, lightly moistened with water.

Your finished rice should be subtly flavored, free of any clumps and firm but tender, never mushy.

2 cups	water	500 mL
2 cups	sushi rice	500 mL
1	piece (4 inches/10 cm) *konbu* (see page 21), optional	1
½	batch Sushi Vinegar (*Awasezu*; page 141)	½

VARIATION

Brown Sushi Rice: Follow the method for making sushi rice, substituting an equal quantity of brown Japonica rice (*genmai*) for the white.

After you have finished washing the rice, fill the bowl with water and set aside for at least 2 hours or overnight to soak. If soaking overnight, refrigerate. It is important to soak brown rice to ensure that water penetrates the bran layer. Otherwise the grains will cook unevenly.

Drain rice and transfer to a saucepan. Add 3 cups (750 mL) water. Bring to a boil over medium heat. Reduce heat to low, cover with a tight-fitting lid and cook for 30 minutes. Remove from heat and let sit, covered, for 15 minutes to absorb any remaining liquid. Your rice is now ready to season for sushi.

▲ Place rice in sieve and place sieve over bowl. Rinse thoroughly with running water, swishing rice gently with your hands.

▲ Drain water and repeat rinsing 4 or 5 times, until water becomes almost clear. Set rice aside for at least 10 minutes and up to 30 minutes to drain thoroughly.

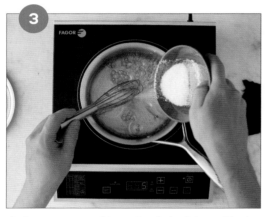

▲ In saucepan, combine water, drained rice and *konbu*, if using. Cover and bring to a boil over medium heat. Boil for 5 minutes, reduce heat and simmer for 15 minutes.

▲ Remove from heat and set aside for 10 to 15 minutes to rest then transfer rice all at once to *hangiri* (rice should be steaming hot).

▲ Using the paddle spread out the rice.

▲ Gently pour sushi vinegar over *shamoji* or spatula so it cascades evenly over surface of rice.

▲ Using rice paddle and working quickly, gently fold vinegar into rice. Fan the rice as you fold.

▲ Finish with the rice pushed to one side of the bowl.

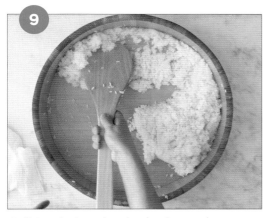

▲ Using a horizontal motion, break up any lumps to ensure that each grain of rice is coated with vinegar. If possible, simultaneously fan rice to help it cool.

▲ Evenly distribute rice in *hangiri* so it is flat. Set aside until cooled to room temperature.

▲ Once rice is no longer steaming, gently flip it over. Set aside until completely cooled. (If desired, use fan.)

▲ Transfer rice to a bowl and cover with a damp kitchen towel for up to 6 hours; if setting aside for longer, refrigerate (bring to room temperature before using).

Hand-Shaped Sushi (*Nigiri*)

HAND-SHAPED SUSHI (*nigiri*)—a bite-size, hand-formed ball of seasoned rice topped with fish—is what most people think of when they think of sushi. Invented in the early 1800s, it was Tokyo's answer to fast food. Up until then, pressed sushi (*oshizushi*, see pages 178 to 182) was eaten at outdoor stalls, but it took a while for the vendors to make it. A chef named Yohei Hanaya decided to skip the pressing. He simply made rice balls and placed a fish on top. His idea caught on, he quickly garnered followers and imitators, and his Edo-style *nigirizushi* eventually spread throughout Japan.

As simple as it sounds, *nigiri* is one of the hardest styles to master in sushi making. It requires some repetition to get the hang of it: apprentice sushi chefs practice by making hundreds of rice balls a day.

When first learning the technique, it is best to practice with a piece of cooked shrimp; you can reuse the shrimp when you form new rice balls and so not waste any fish. Once you become a bit more accomplished, you can expand to using other types of fish, such as tuna, salmon, yellowtail and white fish.

There are several different techniques for making hand-shaped sushi: the flip (*yokotegaeshi*), the roll (*kotegaeshi*) and battleship-style (*gunkanmaki*; see page 155). Here we discuss the flip and the roll (see Tips, page 149).

How to Use Nori to Secure Toppings

Some toppings, if they are firm (such as *tamago* or king crab leg) or slippery (such as clam or scallop), will require the help of a small piece of nori to secure them on top of the rice. To do this, cut a piece of nori about $1/2$ inch (1 cm) wide and 3 inches (7.5 cm) long (or long enough to accommodate the topping). Wrap the nori crosswise around the center of the fish and rice, positioning the ends underneath the sushi, and use a grain of sushi rice to seal.

EATING SUSHI

Sushi can be enjoyed in a few different ways—it is up to personal choice. You may eat sushi with your fingers or using chopsticks. (On the other hand, sashimi should always be eaten with chopsticks.)

Start by pouring a small amount of soy sauce into the soy sauce dish. Try not to pour in so much that you'll be drowning the sushi in soy.

Sushi is meant to be eaten one bite! If you bite a piece of sushi in half, most likely it will fall apart. Then you won't be able to appreciate the delicious combined flavors of fish, rice, wasabi and soy sauce. When eating *nigiri* sushi with your fingers, gently pick up the piece with index and middle fingers and thumb. Dip the topping side into the soy sauce, and then place it directly in your mouth, eaten in one bite.

Hand-Shaped Sushi *Nigiri*

This is the basic technique for making *nigiri*. But even though it's somewhat basic, it will require a lot of practice. Until you master hand-shaping the sushi rice, it's best to limit the types of fish you practice with, to avoid any waste. Preslice the fish using the *sogizukuri* technique (see page 119) before beginning the recipe.

MAKES 20 PIECES

EQUIPMENT

- Wet towel
- Nonstick gloves, optional (see page 95)
- Small bowl with ice water (see Tips, page 192)

TIPS

Any type of high-quality fish (see page 55) can be used to make *nigiri*. Tuna, salmon, yellowtail and white fish are all excellent to use if you are a beginner. Once you become more proficient, you can try flatfish and shellfish.

To make these using the roll method (*kotegaeshi*), in Step 9 use the fingers of your guide hand to roll over the sushi so that it is fish side up.

When making *nigiri*, you will need to rewet your hands repeatedly to prevent sticking. If you prefer, use nonstick gloves (see page 95).

Flip Method (*Yokotegaeshi*)

2 cups	Sushi Rice (page 143), divided	500 mL
20	pieces sushi fish (about 1 lb/500 g), sliced *sogizukuri*-style (see page 119)	20
Dab	wasabi paste	Dab
	Pickled ginger (*Gari*; page 27)	
	Wasabi paste	
	Soy sauce	

VARIATIONS

Don't limit yourself to fish. Raw, cooked or pickled vegetables—such as thinly sliced cucumber or shaved zucchini, grilled sliced zucchini or Japanese eggplant, grilled asparagus, roasted bell peppers, confit of tomato, Japanese pickled plum (*umeboshi*)—and raw or seared meats (such as Kobe beef or foie gras) also make delicious sushi. These ingredients should be cut to roughly the same size and shape as you would cut fish for *nigiri*. For ingredients that won't stay on top of the rice easily, use a small piece of nori to secure them in place (see page 147). You can use a dab of wasabi as you would with fish, or omit it if you don't think the flavor will complement your choice of topping.

For vegetarian sushi: Try using pickled vegetables found at Japanese supermarkets, such as cucumber (*kyūri*), eggplant (*nasu*), burdock root (*gobo*), daikon radish (*takuan*), ginger shallot (*myōga*) or Japanese turnip (*kabu*). You can also use fresh or lightly blanched daikon sprouts (*kaiware*). In fact, you can use any vegetable you have on hand, as long as it will stay on top of the rice (although you can use a piece of nori to help; see page 147).

When describing nigiri, *the topping is referred to as the* neta *and the rice is called the* shari.

TIPS

Throughout this book we use the terms *knife hand* and *guide hand*. Your knife hand naturally holds the knife, while your guide hand holds the food you're cutting. Your dominant hand should be your knife hand.

In the following photos, Robby's knife hand is his left hand. If you are right handed, you may have to reverse the position of your hands.

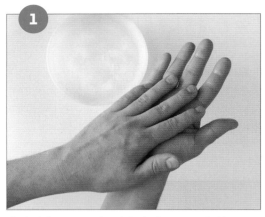

▲ Lightly wet your hands in the ice water, shaking or clapping off any excess (see Tips, page 149).

▲ Pick up about 1 tbsp (15 mL) sushi rice in your knife hand.

▲ Lightly shape it into an oblong—do not squeeze the rice, as that will make it too tight and chewy and unpleasant to eat.

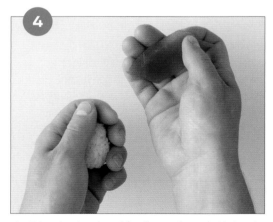

▲ Using the thumb and forefinger of your guide hand, pick up the fish and rest it across the other three fingers of the same hand.

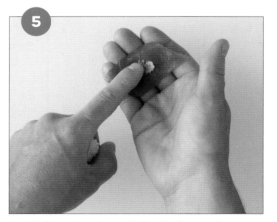

▲ While cupping the rice ball in the fingers of your cutting hand, dab some wasabi on the fish, using the forefinger of the same hand.

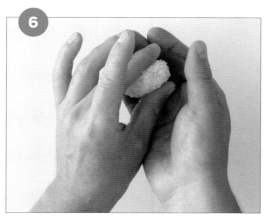

▲ Place the rice on top of the fish in your guide hand.

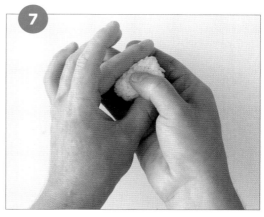

▲ Gently place the thumb of your guide hand on the center of the rice, and the thumb and forefinger of the other hand on the ends of the rice.

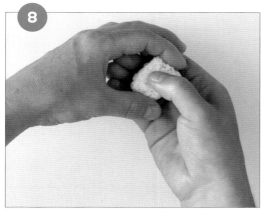

▲ Lightly press, making a slight indentation in the top of the rice with your guide thumb and setting the length with the thumb and forefinger of your knife hand.

▲ Cupping your guide hand slightly, lightly squeeze the sushi between the palm and the first knuckles of your guide hand.

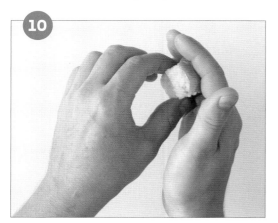

▲ Open your guide hand and, using your knife hand, flip over the sushi so the fish is on top.

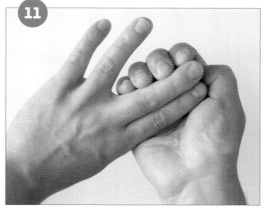

▲ Lightly press down on fish with middle and forefinger of knife hand while simultaneously gently cupping in guide hand and setting the length with the thumb.

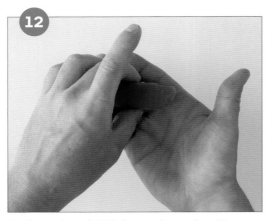

▲ Rotate the sushi 180 degrees. Repeat Step 12, pressing down on the fish. Place finished *nigiri* on cutting board. Repeat process with remaining rice and fish.

▲ Arrange *nigiri* on a serving plate. Garnish with additional wasabi, ginger and a small dipping bowl of soy sauce.

TEMPERATURE MATTERS

When making *nigiri*, it is important to work quickly. If you go too slowly, you will transfer too much body heat to the fish and rice, which will make it too warm for serving (sushi should be served at room temperature). This is why it is best to practice making rice balls without the fish, until you develop comfort and speed.

Battleship Sushi (*Gunkanmaki*)

BATTLESHIP SUSHI (*gunkanmaki*) is a hybrid between hand-shaped sushi (*nigiri*) and rolls (*maki*). A small piece of nori is wrapped around a pad of sushi rice to form an oval cup for loose toppings, which won't stay on the sushi rice without the help of the nori. Traditional toppings include sea urchin (*uni*), salmon roe (*ikura*), flying fish roe (*tobiko*) and spicy cod roe (*mentaiko*), but once you have mastered the basic technique, you can experiment with other toppings such as bay scallops or fermented soybeans (*natto*).

Gunkanmaki gets its name from its distinctive shape, which resembles a battleship. A sushi restaurant called Kyubey, in the Ginza district of Tokyo, is often credited with its invention, around 1941.

If you order items such as *gunkanmaki* (battleship rolls) or *temaki* (hand rolls) at a sushi bar, it is best to eat them first, as they will become soggy and the nori will lose its texture as they sit. The most important advice, however, is to take pleasure in your meal. Follow the basic guidelines, order and eat the sushi you like—and enjoy! This is equally true when you are preparing it at home.

> ## KNIFE/GUIDE HAND
>
> Throughout this book we use the terms *knife hand* and *guide hand*. Your knife hand naturally holds the knife, while your guide hand holds the food you're cutting. Your dominant hand should be your knife hand. In this case it is Robby's left hand; be aware that if you are right-handed, some (but not all) of the positions of the hands in the photos will be reversed.

Flying Fish Roe Battleship Sushi
Tobiko Gunkanmaki

Flying fish roe (*tobiko*) has a great texture—the little eggs pop in your mouth when you bite into them. *Tobiko* comes in a variety of colors: red, black, orange, yellow and green. Some are also infused with wasabi or yuzu for a kick of flavor. When different colors are used and the individual pieces are presented together on a serving plate, or even arranged side by side on a single piece of *gunkanmaki*, the presentation is quite beautiful.

MAKES 3 PIECES

EQUIPMENT

- Chef's knife, petty knife or kitchen shears
- Small bowl with ice water
- Wet towel
- Nonstick gloves, optional (see page 95)

TIPS

Because the nori will absorb moisture from the rice and toppings, *gunkanmaki* should be the last pieces made for a plate of assorted sushi and the first pieces to be eaten.

Store leftover cut nori in its original packaging; otherwise it will lose its crispness.

When making *gunkanmaki* you will need to rewet your hands repeatedly to prevent sticking. If you prefer, use nonstick gloves (see page 95).

3 tbsp	Sushi Rice (page 143)	45 mL
½	sheet nori (7 by 4 inches/17.5 by 10 cm; see page 194), cut into 3 equal pieces (see page 161)	½
Dab	wasabi paste	Dab
3 tbsp	flying fish roe (*tobiko*), divided	45 mL
3	free-range quail egg yolks (see page 160), divided	3
	Wasabi paste	
	Pickled ginger (*Gari*; page 27)	
	Soy sauce	

VARIATIONS

Top each *gunkanmaki* with 1 quail egg yolk (see page 160). Replace the flying fish roe (*tobiko*) with sea urchin (*uni*), salmon roe (*ikura*) or spicy cod roe (*mentaiko*).

Instead of nori, wrap the rice in thin strips of cucumber, carrot or daikon. To cut strips suitable for wrapping, use a sharp knife or mandoline. Cut daikon and cucumber *katsuramuki*-style (see page 24). If using carrot or daikon, marinate the strips in sweet vinegar (*amazu*, page 37) for added flavor. To marinate carrot or daikon strips, place in a shallow dish and cover with sweet vinegar; set aside for 10 to 15 minutes, then drain well, discarding marinade.

For a vegetarian version: Top with diced tomato, mushrooms, squash, zucchini, cooked beets or sprouts. Or try cooked corn or peas mixed with a little mayonnaise.

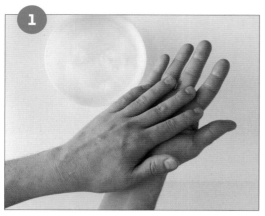

▲ Lightly wet your hands in the ice water, shaking or clapping off any excess (see Tips, page 157).

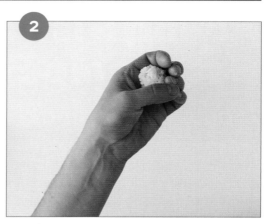

▲ Pick up about 1 tbsp (15 mL) sushi rice in your knife hand. Lightly shape rice into an oblong.

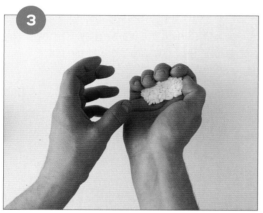

▲ Lightly press, making a slight indentation in the top of the rice with your guide thumb and setting the length with the thumb and forefinger of your knife hand.

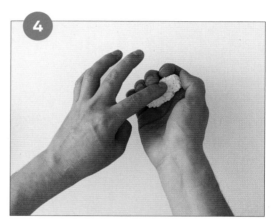

▲ Cupping your guide hand slightly, lightly squeeze the rice between the palm and first knuckles of your guide hand as you begin to complete Step 6.

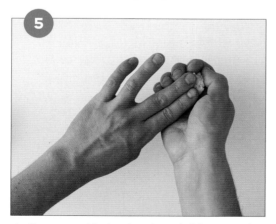

▲ Keep your guide thumb at the end of the rice, and press down lightly with two fingers from your knife hand to form the rice ball.

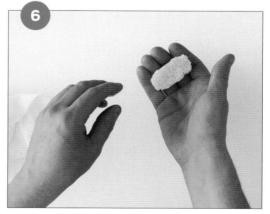

▲ Open your guide hand and, using your knife hand, flip over rice.

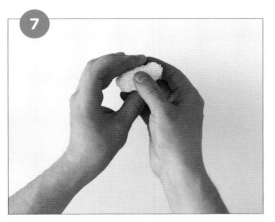

▲ Rotate rice 180 degrees.

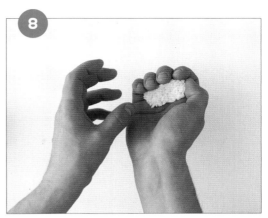

▲ Repeat Steps 5 and 6.

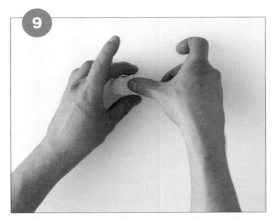

▲ Place rice ball on cutting board. Gently place the thumb of your guide hand on the center of the rice, and the thumb and middle finger of your knife hand on either side of the rice, to make a slight indentation for the filling.

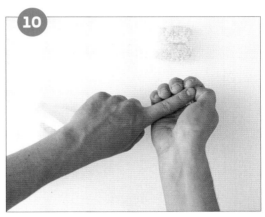

▲ Repeat the process (Steps 1 to 9) two more times to create a total of 3 balls of rice.

TIP

When forming the rice balls, do not squeeze the rice, as this will make it too tight and chewy, and thus unpleasant to eat.

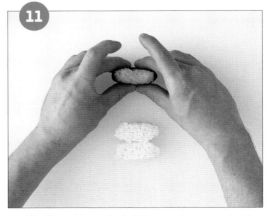

▲ Working with one ball of rice at a time, wrap 1 strip of nori around the length of the rice (to form a ring), using a single grain of sushi rice to seal nori.

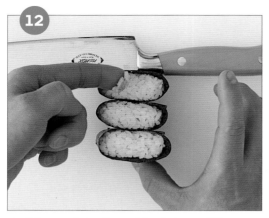

▲ Using your index finger, dab a little wasabi in center of rice and gently flatten rice.

▲ Spoon 1 tbsp (15 mL) flying fish roe inside each ring of nori. Rest your knife against the roll to help seal the nori.

▲ To serve, arrange *gunkanmaki* on a plate with wasabi, pickled ginger and a small dipping bowl of soy sauce.

▲ *Tobiko Gunkanmaki Topped with Quail Egg Yolks:* Using the back of a spoon, make a slight indentation in the roe at the end closest to you. Gently place a quail egg yolk in the indentation.

QUAIL EGGS

Quail eggs can be found at well-stocked grocers, butchers and Asian markets. They can be separated into yolk and white just as you would a chicken's egg, but they cannot be cracked similarly. To crack and separate quail eggs, hold the egg with the narrower end pointing down. Using a sharp knife or a small serrated one, slice off the top of the shell. Pour the contents into your hand. Let the white slide through your fingers and into a bowl and retain the yolk in your fingers.

Cutting Nori for Battleship Rolls (*Gunkanmaki*)

Cut the nori before beginning the recipe. One half-sheet of nori will yield 3 strips suitable for battleship sushi (*gunkanmaki*) and 2 smaller strips that can be used to wrap hand-shaped sushi (*nigiri*).

▲ Place nori on cutting board with the longer side facing you (make sure cutting board is completely dry to prevent nori from becoming soggy).

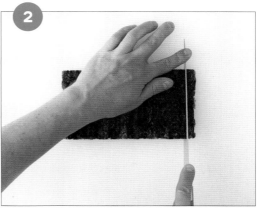

▲ Using a sharp knife and starting ½ inch (1 cm) from right edge of nori, place your index finger on tip of the knife and cut down swiftly through nori.

▲ Set aside strip and repeat Step 2. Reserve strips for use on *nigiri*.

▲ Rotate remaining nori 90 degrees and cut into 3 equal pieces, each about 1¼ inches (3 cm) wide. These can be used to make *gunkanmaki*.

Scattered Sushi (*Chirashi*)

SCATTERED SUSHI (*chirashi*) evolved as a special-occasion dish sometime during the Edo period (1600–1800). Today it is one of the easiest types of sushi to prepare and is often served as a quick meal in Japanese homes. Typically, assorted raw fish and pickled and cooked vegetables are artfully arranged in a bowl over a bed of sushi rice and garnished with rolled omelet (*tamago*), nori and green onions; however, vegetarian versions are popular as well.

When preparing *chirashi*, a wide, shallow bowl about 7¾ inches (20 cm) in diameter and 2¾ inches (7 cm) in depth is preferred, but any shallow bowl will do—just remember, the larger the surface area of the rice, the more toppings you will need to cover the space. If you prefer, the toppings can be mixed into the rice so the combined flavors can be experienced all in one bite.

For the Japanese, color is a very important component in the presentation of *chirashi*. The assortment of toppings should include a good balance of the five primary colors of Japanese cuisine: red, yellow, green, black and white. For example, use tuna, salmon and shrimp for red; *tamago* for yellow; wasabi, bamboo shoots and shiso leaf for green; nori and black sesame seeds for black; and sushi rice and white sesame seeds for white.

Chirashi Styles

There are several different styles of chirashi:

- **Tokyo- or Edo-style *chirashi*:** This style is known for its abundance of ingredients, picked as much for how they look together in the bowl as for how they taste together. Slices of raw fish are decoratively arranged on top of sushi rice, with colors alternating to make a beautiful presentation.
- ***Bara chirashi*:** This style is similar to a rice salad. Cubed raw fish is quickly marinated in soy sauce and scattered over the sushi rice, then garnished with pickled vegetables, rolled omelet (*tamago*), cucumber, salmon roe (*ikura*) and shrimp. You can also mix the ingredients together with the rice.
- ***Gomoku chirashi*:** This is a vegetarian bowl in which cooked veggies are mixed with sushi rice and topped with julienned rolled omelet (*tamago*), and snow peas.

Tokyo-Style Scattered Sushi Edo-Style *Chirashi*

This style of *chirashi* is the most artful of the scattered sushis. Slices of sashimi are carefully arranged on top of sushi rice with the goal of pleasing the eye as well as the stomach.

MAKES 1 BOWL

EQUIPMENT

- *Yanagiba*, slicing knife or chef's knife
- Small bowl with ice water (see Tips, page 192)
- Wet towel
- Serving bowl (see Tips, below)
- Plating chopsticks (*moribashi*), optional

TIPS

Use the *katsuramuki* technique (see page 24) to shred the daikon.

A wide, shallow serving bowl, about 7¾ inches (20 cm) in diameter and 2¾ inches (7 cm) deep, provides the ideal surface area for presentation, but any wide bowl will do. A narrower bowl will limit the amount of toppings you can use.

Using plating chopsticks (*moribashi*; see page 54) to transfer the toppings onto the rice provides greater flexibility and allows you to arrange them more precisely.

The toppings should be arranged artistically for best presentation. In general, place the taller and bolder-colored items in the bowl first, at the back (12 o'clock position).

1 cup	Sushi Rice (page 143)	250 mL
1 tbsp	shredded daikon (see Tips, left)	15 mL
1	shiso leaf	1
3	pieces thick-cut (¼ to ½ inch/0.5 to 1 cm) *hirazukiri*-style tuna (about 2 oz/60 g; see page 103)	3
1	piece thick-cut (¼ to ½ inch/0.5 to 1 cm) *hirazukiri*-style Rolled Omelet (*Tamago*; about 1 oz/30 g; page 32), cut in half on the diagonal	1
2	pieces thick-cut (¼ to ½ inch/0.5 to 1 cm) *hirazukiri*-style yellowtail (about 1 oz/30 g)	2
2	pieces thin-cut (⅛ inch/3 mm) *sogizukuri*-style salmon (about 1 oz/30 g; see page 119)	2
2	pieces thin-cut (⅛ inch/3 mm) *sogizukuri*-style white fish (fluke, snapper or striped bass; about 1 oz/30 g)	2
1	piece sushi shrimp (*ebi*), halved lengthwise (see page 82)	1
1	large scallop (*hotate*; 1 oz/30 g), sliced into ⅛-inch (3 mm) pieces	1
1 tbsp	salmon roe (*ikura*)	15 mL
4	pieces thinly sliced (⅛ inch/3 mm) unpeeled Japanese cucumber	4
	Wasabi paste	
	Pickled ginger (*Gari*; page 27)	
	Soy sauce	

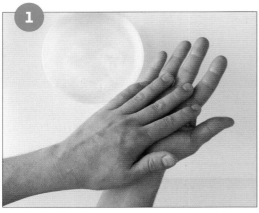

▲ Lightly wet your hands in the ice water, shaking or clapping off any excess.

▲ Place sushi rice in serving bowl and, using your hand, gently pat the top flat without compressing it.

▲ Using the palms of your hands, gently roll daikon into a small ball and place on top of rice in the 12 o'clock position.

▲ Lean shiso leaf against front of daikon ball.

▲ Arrange tuna pieces so they fan out slightly from the daikon and shiso.

▲ To the left of tuna, place *tamago*, long points facing up.

▲ Place yellowtail in front of tuna.

▲ Place salmon in front of *tamago*.

▲ Arrange shrimp in front of salmon.

▲ Arrange scallop in front of shrimp.

▲ Arrange white fish in front of yellowtail.

▲ Fan out cucumber in front of the fish.

▲ Place salmon roe in front of cucumber.

▲ Serve with wasabi, ginger and a small dipping bowl of soy sauce on the side.

VARIATIONS

To make this dish vegetarian: Swap out the fish for more fresh, pickled or cooked vegetables. For example, use halved or chopped cooked shiitake mushrooms, julienned carrots, bean sprouts, thinly sliced (1/8 inch/3 mm) bamboo shoots, Japanese pickled plums (*umeboshi*), thinly sliced (1/8 inch/3 mm) pickled daikon radish (*takuan*), blanched asparagus, or cooked or raw baby spinach.

During the Edo period, people would sometimes build this chirashi *upside down, with the toppings underneath the rice. The dish would then be flipped over upon serving to reveal the ingredients.*

TIPS

Some people add the vinegar from pickled ginger to the ice water used for wetting your hands to help prevent bacterial growth.

Wetting your hands helps to prevent sticking. If you prefer, use nonstick gloves.

Scattered-Style Sushi
Bara Chirashi

In this type of scattered sushi, cubed raw fish is scattered over a bowl of sushi rice. You can use the same ingredients as you would when making Tokyo-Style *Chirashi* (page 165).

MAKES 1 BOWL

EQUIPMENT

- *Yanagiba,* slicing knife or chef's knife
- Small bowl with ice water (see Tips, page 192)
- Wet towel
- Serving bowl (see Tips, below)
- Small mixing bowl

TIPS

We recommend cutting the ingredients into ½-inch (1 cm) cubes, but you can cut them smaller or larger as desired.

A wide, shallow serving bowl, about 7¾ inches (20 cm) in diameter and 2¾ inches (7 cm) deep, will give you the ideal surface area for presentation. If you don't have one, any wide bowl will do. Just keep in mind that a narrower bowl will limit the amount of toppings you can use.

If desired, gently stir together the toppings and rice (like a rice salad) rather than layering them one on top of the other.

For even more flavor, stir diced pickled vegetables, such as lotus root and Japanese ginger (myōga; available at Japanese markets), into your rice.

1 cup	Sushi Rice (page 143)	250 mL
	Toasted sesame seeds (preferably a mix of black and white)	
½	sheet nori (7 by 4 inches/17.5 by 10 cm; see page 194)	½
3	pieces tuna (about 2 oz/60 g), cut into ½-inch (1 cm) cubes	3
2	pieces salmon (about 1 oz/30 g), cut into ½-inch (1 cm) cubes	2
2	pieces yellowtail (about 1 oz/30 g), cut into ½-inch (1 cm) cubes	2
2	pieces white fish (fluke, snapper or striped bass; about 1 oz/30 g), cut into ½-inch (1 cm) cubes	2
1	scallop (1 oz/30 g), cut into ¼-inch (0.5 cm) cubes	1
1 tbsp	soy sauce	15 mL
1	thin (½ inch/1 cm thick) Rolled Omelet (*Tamago*; page 32), cut into ½-inch (1 cm) cubes	1
1	piece sushi shrimp, diced (see page 82)	1
1	2-inch (5 cm) piece unpeeled Japanese cucumber, cut into ½-inch (1 cm) cubes	1
1 tbsp	salmon roe (*ikura*)	15 mL
	Wasabi paste	
	Pickled ginger (*Gari*; page 27)	
	Additional soy sauce, for serving	

This style of chirashi doesn't require the precision of the Edo style. It's much quicker to prepare.

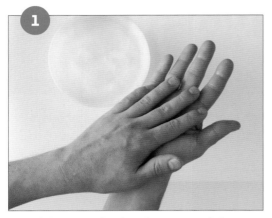

▲ Lightly wet your hands in the ice water, shaking or clapping off any excess (see Tips, page 168).

▲ Place sushi rice in serving bowl and, using your hand, gently pat the top flat without compressing it.

▲ Sprinkle sesame seeds evenly over rice.

▲ Crumble nori evenly over sesame seeds.

▲ In mixing bowl, combine all of the fish and soy sauce, stirring gently until well coated. Let marinate for 1 minute.

▲ Scatter marinated fish in a thick, even layer over nori, covering surface completely.

▲ Scatter *tamago*, shrimp and cucumber evenly overtop. Sprinkle with salmon roe.

▲ Serve with wasabi, ginger and a small dipping bowl of soy sauce on the side.

Vegetarian Scattered Sushi *Gomoku Chirashi*

In this style of scattered sushi, which is akin to a rice salad, cooked vegetables are mixed with rice and garnished with *tamago* and nori. This very versatile dish works equally well as a portable lunch or picnic as it does as a light dinner.

MAKES 1 BOWL

EQUIPMENT

- Chef's knife
- Small mixing bowl
- Serving bowl (see Tips, below)

TIPS

A wide, shallow serving bowl about 7¾ inches (20 cm) in diameter and 2¾ inches (7 cm) deep, will give you the ideal surface area for presentation. If you don't have one, any wide bowl will do. Just keep in mind that a narrower bowl will limit the amount of toppings you can use.

If your mushroom caps are large, use 4; if they are smaller in size, use 6.

You can use store-bought pre-shredded nori or use kitchen scissors to chiffonade (cut into fine shreds) sheets of nori.

To save time, look for packages of sliced lotus root and pickled vegetables at Asian grocers.

This dish comes together quickly when you prepare all the ingredients before assembling the dish.

1 cup	Sushi Rice (page 143)	250 mL
4 to 6	shiitake mushroom caps, thinly sliced (see Tips, left)	4 to 6
2 tbsp	chopped pickled gourd (*kanpyō*, see page 36)	30 mL
1	piece deep-fried tofu pouch (*inari*), thinly sliced	1
1	3-inch (7.5 cm) piece pickled burdock root (*gobō*), julienned	1
1	lotus root (2 oz/30 g), thinly sliced (reserve 2 slices for garnish)	1
8	snow peas, blanched and julienned (reserve 2 whole snow peas for garnish)	8
	Toasted sesame seeds (preferably a mix of black and white)	
1 tbsp	shredded nori (see Tips, left)	15 mL
2	thin (½ inch/1 cm thick) Rolled Omelets (*Tamago*; see page 32), julienned	2
	Additional shredded nori, for garnish	
	Wasabi paste	
	Pickled ginger (*Gari*; page 27)	
	Soy sauce	

VARIATIONS

Substitute about 2 tbsp to ¼ cup (30 to 60 mL) each blanched asparagus, cooked carrot and squash and enoki or *matsutake* mushrooms for the snow peas, pickled gourd, pickled burdock root, lotus root and shiitakes. Replace the vegetables called for with any seasonal local vegetables.

▲ In mixing bowl, combine rice, shiitakes, pickled gourd, tofu pouch, burdock root, lotus root, julienned snow peas and sesame seeds. Stir gently to combine.

▲ Transfer mixture to serving bowl. Sprinkle with shredded nori.

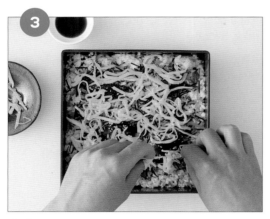

▲ Scatter *tamago* overtop.

▲ Cut reserved snow peas in half on the diagonal and arrange over *tamago*.

▲ Add reserved lotus root. Garnish with a sprinkling of sesame seeds and additional shredded nori.

▲ Serve with wasabi, ginger and a small dipping bowl of soy sauce on the side.

Pressed Sushi (*Oshizushi*)

THE PREDECESSOR to hand-shaped sushi (*nigiri*), box-shaped pressed sushi (*hakozushi*, also often referred to as Osaka-style sushi) is one of the oldest types of sushi. Originating around the 14th century, it was used as a preservation technique. Fish preserved in vinegar and rice were pressed together in a wooden mold (*oshizushihako*, or *hako*) to form a block of sushi, which was then cut up to serve or stored for up to a year. Today *hakozushi* is favored more for presentation and ease of preparation than for preservation. The fish is lightly pickled and meant to be eaten soon after preparation, or refrigerated for just a few days.

The traditional three-piece wooden mold—consisting of top, bottom and sides—can be found at most Japanese supermarkets. You can also find dishwasher-safe plastic molds that may be more nonstick. If you can't find a mold, you can improvise with a 9-inch (23 cm) square baking pan lined with plastic wrap, plus a second pan for pressing.

Stick sushi (*bouzushi*) is another type of pressed sushi. Rather than being assembled in a mold, *bouzushi* is formed into a log with your hands and then rolled with a cloth and rolling mat. It is known as "stick" sushi because before cutting it resembles a large stick or log. Originating in Kyoto, an inland city, around the same time as *hakozushi*, it was a style favored for preserving fish for the long journey from the sea.

Today pressed sushi (*oshizushi*), as these two styles are called, is usually made with salt-cured and vinegar-marinated mackerel. In Japan it is often wrapped in bamboo leaves and is a popular takeout food for parties, gifts and souvenirs.

Pressed sushi is best made a few hours in advance so the flavors of the rice and toppings have time to develop. This makes it great for entertaining. Wrap the unmolded sushi block in plastic wrap and refrigerate until ready to serve (bring to room temperature before serving). When ready to serve, slice the sushi crosswise into 8 small pieces. Garnish with sliced *sudachi* (see page 28), grated ginger and green onions, or sweet vinegared seaweed/*konbu*.

Sushi Rice with Ginger

You can also make *oshizushi* with sushi rice seasoned with ginger. On a chopping board, combine 2 tbsp (30 mL) pickled ginger (*Gari*, page 27) and 1 tsp (5 mL) toasted sesame seeds (preferably a mix of white and black). Finely chop together to blend flavors; set aside. Finely chop 2 shiso leaves. Add ginger mixture and shiso to a bowl with 1½ cups (375 mL) Sushi Rice (page 143) and stir until well incorporated.

Cured Mackerel Box-Shaped Pressed Sushi Mackerel *Hakozushi*

Boxed sushi (*hakozushi*) is made by using a three-piece wooden mold called an *oshizushihako*, or *hako*. It's easy and fun to make and yields perfect little pieces. Since it can be made in advance (see Tips, page 182), it's great for parties.

MAKES 1 *HAKOZUSHI* (8 PIECES)

EQUIPMENT

- Wooden or plastic sushi mold (*hako*; see page 54 and Tips, below)
- Wet towel
- Nonstick gloves, optional (see page 95)
- Small bowl with ice water
- *Yanagiba*, slicing knife or chef's knife (see Slicing Rolls, page 192)

TIPS

If using a wooden mold, soak it in water for 10 minutes before using to help prevent rice from sticking to the walls and bottom of the mold and to make releasing the mold easier. Thoroughly dry the soaked mold before using.

If you find that the rice and fish stick to the mold, line the top and bottom with bamboo leaves (see page 28) or wax paper.

1½ cups	Sushi Rice (page 143)	375 mL
1	fillet cured mackerel (about 4 oz/125 g; page 289), deboned and skin removed (see Tips, page 182)	1
	Wasabi paste	
	Pickled ginger (*Gari*; page 27)	
	Ponzu or soy sauce	

VARIATIONS

If available, wrap the unmolded sushi block in bamboo leaves (see page 26) and set aside for up to 8 hours before serving. They impart a mild woody flavor, reminiscent of bamboo shoots.

Hakozushi *with Sushi Rice with Ginger:* Substitute an equal amount of Sushi Rice with Ginger (page 178) for the rice.

***Smoked Salmon and Cucumber* Hakozushi:** Substitute 2 oz (60 g) each thinly sliced smoked salmon and cucumber for the mackerel. Arrange in an alternating pattern.

***Marinated Tuna with Wasabi* Furikake Hakozushi:** Substitute 4 oz (60 g) soy-marinated tuna, thinly sliced, for the mackerel. Season with wasabi *furikake* (see page 281) to taste before covering with the lid in Step 5.

***Vegetable* Hakozushi:** Replace the mackerel with about ¼ cup (60 mL) mixed thinly sliced pickled vegetables such as cucumber (*kyūri*), eggplant (*nasu*), daikon radish (*takuan*) or Japanese turnip (*kabu*), or thinly sliced carrot and shiitake mushrooms. Arrange in an alternating pattern.

Other traditional toppings include cooked sushi shrimp (see page 82), soy-braised sea eel (*anago*) and whole fillet of marinated mackerel (*saba*).

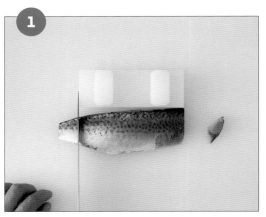

▲ Trim the meat side of the mackerel fillet so it will fit flat in the mold. Reserve trimmings to fill in any gaps around the fish. Set aside.

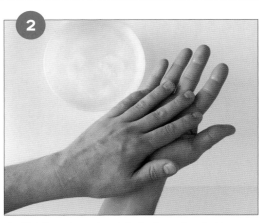

▲ Lightly wet your hands in the ice water, shaking or clapping off any excess, to help prevent sticking.

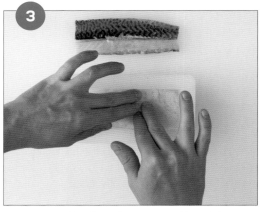

▲ Using your hands, pack rice into mold until about two-thirds full.

▲ Lay trimmed mackerel on top of rice, meat side down. Fill in any gaps with reserved trimmings.

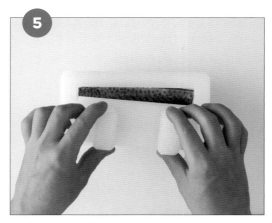

▲ Cover mold with the lid.

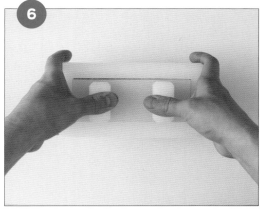

▲ Using your thumbs, gently but firmly press down.

▲ Rotate mold 180 degrees.

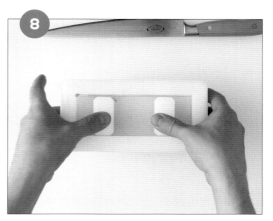

▲ Press down on lid again. Repeat Steps 6, 7 and 8 six times to compact the rice and fish.

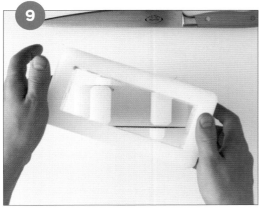

▲ Start to unmold the sushi block by holding down the lid with your thumbs as you lift up the sides of the mold.

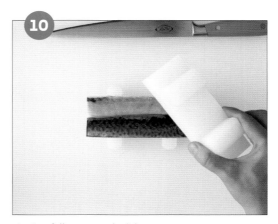

▲ Carefully remove the lid.

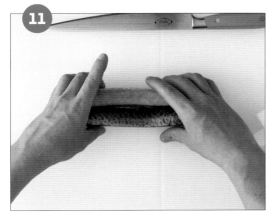

▲ Carefully lift and transfer sushi block to cutting board, leaving behind the bottom of the mold.

▲ Dip the tip of your knife in the ice water, then, in a swift motion, stand the knife up on the end of its handle so the water drips down the edge of the knife.

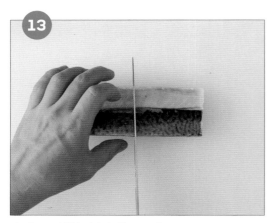

▲ Cut sushi block in half crosswise.

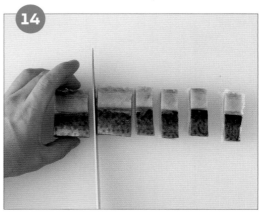

▲ Cut each half into 4 equal pieces, wiping and wetting knife blade after each cut.

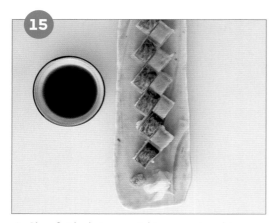

▲ Place finished pieces upright on a serving plate. Garnish with wasabi, ginger and a small dipping bowl of soy sauce.

TIPS

Mackerel has two layers of skin (it has no scales): an outer thin, clear membrane and an inner shiny silver one. To prepare for eating, only the clear membrane is removed. The silver layer is full of flavor and rich in omega-3 fatty acids; it makes for a beautiful presentation and is meant to be eaten.

For a decorative effect, remove the silverskin on one side of the fillet.

Because the fish is cured, the sushi does not need to be refrigerated. Store pressed sushi in an airtight container at room temperature for up to 8 hours.

Some chefs prefer to assemble pressed sushi in reverse, placing the fish in first and packing the rice on top. Experiment to see what you prefer.

You can also include an additional layer of topping in the center of the sushi, so that you have rice–topping–rice–topping.

Stick-Shaped Sushi *Bouzushi*

Stick-shaped sushi is similar to pressed sushi (the same toppings can be used), except that instead of a square or rectangular mold, you use a damp towel or cheesecloth and a bamboo mat to form the sushi into a log or stick. This style of sushi is very popular in Kyoto, where it is traditionally prepared with cured mackerel.

MAKES
1 *BOUZUSHI*
(8 PIECES)

EQUIPMENT

- Cutting board
- *Yanagiba*, slicing knife or chef's knife (see Slicing Rolls, page 192)
- Small bowl with ice water
- Damp towel or cheesecloth
- Bamboo rolling mat (*makisu*)
- Nonstick gloves, optional (see page 95)

TIP

This sushi can be made in advance, wrapped in plastic wrap or bamboo leaves (see page 28) and set aside at room temperature for up to 8 hours or refrigerated for up to 8 days (bring to room temperature before serving). Slice into 8 pieces.

1½ cups	Sushi Rice (page 143)	375 mL
1	fillet cured mackerel (about 4 oz/125 g; page 289), deboned, skin removed and butterflied (see page 188)	1
1 tsp	finely grated peeled gingerroot	5 mL
1 tsp	finely sliced green onion	5 mL
	Wasabi paste	
	Pickled ginger (*Gari*; page 27)	
	Ponzu or soy sauce	

VARIATIONS

Snow Crab Bouzushi *with Sushi Rice with Ginger:* Replace the sushi rice with Sushi Rice with Ginger (page 178). Proceed with Step 1. In Step 4, lay 3 to 4 crab legs side by side, then proceed with the recipe.

Rainbow Roll–Style Bouzushi*:* Prepare fish as specified in the Rainbow Roll recipe (page 247). Reduce the amount of sushi rice to about 1 cup (250 mL). In Step 4, arrange the fish as you would for the top of a rainbow roll (see Step 1, page 248), but instead of placing the fish on rice, place it directly on the cloth. Proceed with Step 5.

After completing Step 4, add chopped sushi ginger and shiso. Then add the rice (Step 5).

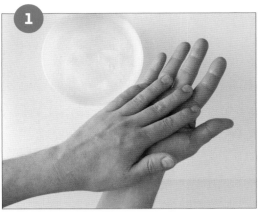

▲ Lightly wet your hands in the ice water, shaking or clapping off any excess.

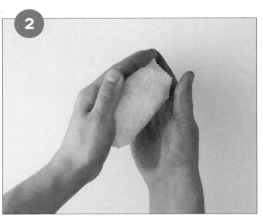

▲ Using your hands, form the sushi rice into a cylinder about the same length as the mackerel, pressing firmly so the rice sticks together. Set aside.

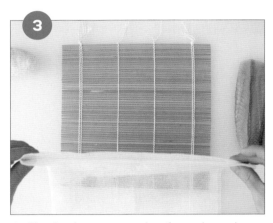

▲ Place bamboo mat on work surface and spread damp cloth overtop.

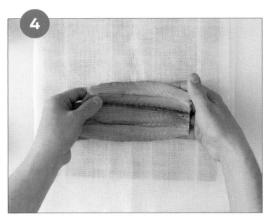

▲ Lay mackerel fillet along center of damp cloth.

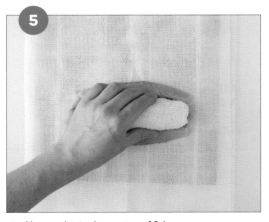

▲ Place sushi rice log on top of fish.

▲ Fold one side of cloth over fish and rice.

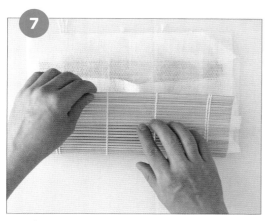

▲ Lift mat over roll.

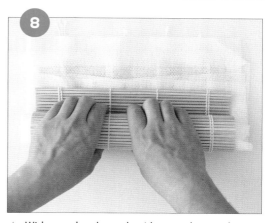

▲ With your thumbs on the side toward you and your other fingers cupped over the top, press firmly to shape into a log, tucking in ends of rice and fish.

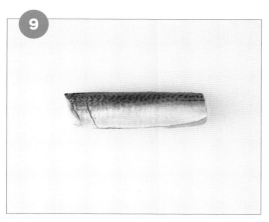

▲ Remove mat, unwrap cloth and place sushi, fish side up, on cutting board.

▲ Dip the tip of your knife in the ice water, then, in a swift motion, stand the knife up on the end of its handle so the water drips down the edge of the knife.

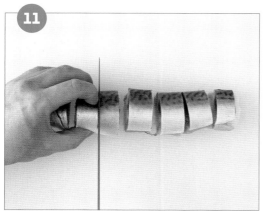

▲ Slice sushi into 8 pieces, wiping the knife blade clean and rewetting after each cut so rice doesn't stick.

▲ Arrange cut pieces upright on a serving plate. Garnish each piece with ginger and green onions.

How to Butterfly a Fillet

Butterflying a fish fillet before making log-shaped sushi (*bouzushi*) will make it easier for you to wrap the fish around the rice.

<table>
<tr><td>

EQUIPMENT

- Chef's knife or slicer (see page 43)

</td><td>1</td><td>fillet cured mackerel</td><td>1</td></tr>
</table>

▲ Lay fillet lengthwise on cutting board, with the tail end toward you. Locate the lateral line (see page 57).

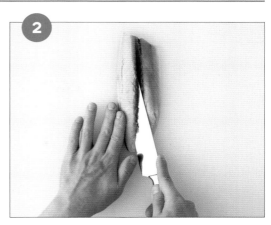

▲ Holding your knife almost parallel to the board and with your forefinger extended along spine of knife, line up the blade on one side of the lateral line.

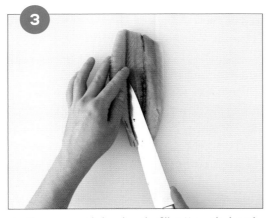

▲ Place your guide hand on the fillet. Using the length of your blade, slice into the fish away from the line— about halfway through the thickness of the fillet.

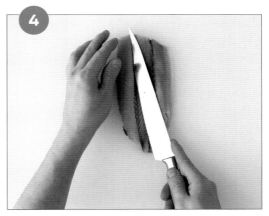

▲ Continue cutting fillet in broad strokes, stopping just before you cut all the way through.

▲ Turn fillet 180 degrees so tail end is facing away from you.

▲ Repeat Steps 2 to 4 until you have opened up the other side.

Rolled Sushi (*Makizushi*)

MAKI MEANS "ROLL," so *makizushi* is "rolled sushi." Rolled sushi originated in Japan around the late 19th century as a way for customers to keep their hands clean while eating sushi from street carts.

Rolls are one of the most popular aspects of sushi—everywhere except Japan. There, hand-shaped sushi (*nigiri*) and sliced raw fish (sashimi) are king. For the most part, sushi is rolled in seaweed (nori), making it *norimaki*, or "rolled seaweed." Traditional sushi rolls have the seaweed on the outside; if the rice is on the outside they are considered "inside-out rolls" (*uramaki*), which were invented in North America (see below).

Rolled sushi and its variations can be stuffed with strips of assorted seafood, fresh or pickled vegetables, and garnishes such as toasted sesame seeds and fish roe. The fillings, either on their own or in flavorful combinations, are arranged on vinegared rice (*shari*) that has been evenly spread onto sheets of nori. The ingredients are rolled and then sliced into individual pieces for serving. Usually rolls are cut into six pieces.

Rolled sushi falls into four basic categories: small rolls (*hosomaki*), large rolls (*futomaki*), inside-out rolls (*uramaki*) and hand rolls (*temaki*). In this chapter we also include some decorative rolls, as well as rolls wrapped in vegetables rather than seaweed.

Small rolls (*hosomaki*) are the most traditional types of rolls. They are the first rolls apprentice chefs learn how to make. Small rolls require half a sheet of nori (see page 20) and contain only one or two ingredients, the second of which is usually a garnish. Finished rolls are usually no more than 1 inch (2.5 cm) wide.

The global popularity of sushi that started in the 1960s can be traced back to the invention of inside-out rolls (*uramaki*) in the United States. They are called inside-out rolls because the sushi rice is on the outside of the roll while the nori is hidden inside. These Western-style sushi rolls are popular because of the wide assortment of ingredients that can be used as fillings. In addition to raw fish, the inclusion of fried items such as shrimp, crab or vegetable tempura and assorted sauces such as mayonnaise (spicy or plain) makes these rolls appealing.

Inside-out rolls are a little easier to make than other rolls because the rice helps the roll stick together. Another advantage is that inside-out rolls can be made ahead of time and refrigerated, since it is less important for the nori to be crispy.

Large rolls (*futomaki*) combine a variety of flavors, textures and colors. They require a full sheet of nori and are usually about 2 to 2.5 inches (5 to 6 cm) in diameter, which allows for more ingredients. These are great rolls to serve at parties. Once you've mastered the technique, you can experiment with an endless variety of ingredients.

Hand-rolled sushi (*temaki*) is executed completely with your hands, not on the cutting board or mat (*makisu*). Ingredients are similar to those used to make small rolls (*hosomaki*) and inside-out rolls (*uramaki*). The rolls can be formed in the shape of a cone or cylinder, depending on preference (we show you how to do both). Hand-rolled sushi also make a great party appetizer or fun family dinner: you can put a platter of assorted fillings and sushi rice on the table and let everyone choose their own fillings and make their own sushi.

Once you gain confidence by mastering basic sushi-making techniques, you may want to try your hand at something a little more difficult.

Decorative rolls (*kazaramaki*) are fancy shaped rolls that sushi chefs use to show off their skills. There are endless variations; we have included two of our favorites—a teardrop roll and a square roll. Either of these will give your presentations a wow factor. In case you are feeding people who are seaweed averse, we'll also show you how to make vegetable-wrapped rolls as an alternative to nori.

Rolled sushi makes a fun and creative way to present a meal. Despite its simplicity, however, rolling sushi does require practice to master. We've arranged this chapter from simpler to more complicated rolls, and we recommend that you practice and become confident with making the first (cucumber roll/ *kappamaki*) before you move on to other, more challenging rolls.

Slicing Rolls (*Maki*)

All types of rolls (*maki*)—with the exception of hand rolls (*temaki*)—are sliced in the same manner. A *yanagiba* (see page 40) is the best knife for this task.

MAKES 1 ROLL (6 PIECES)

EQUIPMENT

- *Yanagiba,* slicing knife or chef's knife
- Small bowl with ice water

Some people add the vinegar from pickled ginger to the ice water used for wetting their hands and knife to help prevent bacterial growth.

VARIATIONS

You can also cut a roll into 8 pieces by cutting the roll in half, then cutting the 2 resulting pieces in half, and finally cutting the 4 remaining pieces in half or, in the case of the Spider Roll, into 5 even pieces.

TIPS

Wetting the knife (Step 1) helps to prevent sticking and catching. After every cut, wipe clean and rewet your knife.

Rewet your hands to prevent the rice from sticking. Clap them together to remove excess water (this will help to keep the nori dry).

▲ Dip the tip of your knife in water, then stand the knife up on the end of its handle in a swift motion so that the water drips down the edge of the blade.

▲ Place your forefinger on the spine of the knife.

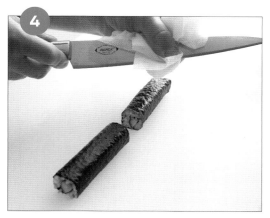

▲ Using the top one-third of the knife and a slight rocking motion, slice the roll in half.

▲ Wipe your knife with a wet towel and then repeat Step 1.

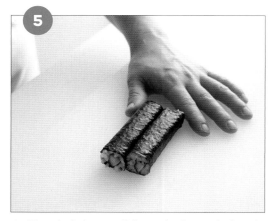

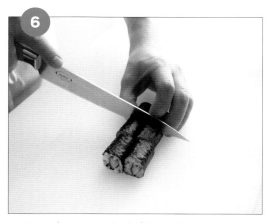

▲ Place the halves parallel to each other on the board.

▲ Using the top one-third of the knife and a slight rocking motion, slice both halves into thirds, wiping and rewetting the knife between cuts.

Dry Toasted Seaweed (Nori)

NORI IS A TYPE of dry toasted seaweed (sometimes called "purple laver," a marine alga) used to make sushi rolls (*maki*). It is also used to prepare battleship sushi (*gunkanmaki*) and, when crumbled and sprinkled over sushi rice, is a garnish for scattered sushi (*chirashi*). Nori is probably the best-known of all the seaweeds because of the popularity of sushi.

Today the majority of nori is farm-raised in Hokkaido, Japan. Spores are attached to nets laid out in calm bays and left to grow. They are ready for harvesting about 45 days after seeding; multiple harvests are taken from a single planting, usually every 10 days after the first. The practice is similar to oyster farming. The traditional process of making nori resembles papermaking. The seaweed is collected, spread thinly over mesh sheets and allowed to dry. It is then toasted and sheeted on what looks like a printing press.

Dry toasted nori is sold in standard 8- by 7-inch (20 by 17.5 cm) sheets and should be green-black in color. The sheets should be crisp, with one shiny side and one tight-grained, slightly rough side. The nori should have a crisp, dry texture and dissolve in your mouth. If it is dull and chewy, it is either of poor quality or old and shouldn't be used for sushi (instead, you can chop it into pieces and add it to soups).

Nori is usually sold in packs of 10 sheets. As with most things, price is a good indicator of quality. At the sushi bar we store them in tin boxes to keep them crisp. Some of the more expensive brands come already packaged in a tin box. Once a package of nori is opened, it is best to use it as quickly as possible. Moisture in the air causes nori to become flimsy and lose its flavor. For this reason it is often packed with a packet of desiccant (drying agent).

TOASTING NORI

Toasting nori over a flame before using will improve its flavor and texture. To toast nori, hold it between two fingers and gently wave the sheet from side to side over a low gas or charcoal flame for a few seconds until it becomes crisp (be careful not to tear the nori). You can also use a mini torch, such as the kind you use to make crème brûlée, or purchase a Japanese grill (*konro*, pictured below), which burns Japanese charcoal (*binchotan*), a very hard and hot-burning premium charcoal.

HOW TO CUT HALF-SHEETS OF NORI

Most Japanese supermarkets sell half-sheets of nori (7 by 4 inches/ 17.5 by 10 cm). If you cannot find half-sheets, it's easy to cut full sheets to size: Gently and neatly fold a full sheet of nori in half lengthwise. Using your fingertips, pinch along the folded edge and then gently break the sheet apart into two pieces. If you prefer, you can use sharp kitchen shears.

Cucumber Roll *Kappamaki*

Cucumber rolls are the first type of roll an apprentice sushi chef learns to make. Cucumber is usually the least expensive ingredient for the restaurant. For practice, some restaurants go as far as using cucumber scraps, leftover rice and lower-priced nori. Once you have mastered this type of rolled sushi, other types will be much easier to execute. We recommend that you practice by making a lot of cucumber rolls before moving on to those that are more complicated. It will help you to become comfortable with the techniques before tackling more expensive ingredients.

MAKES 1 ROLL (6 PIECES)

EQUIPMENT

- Vegetable peeler
- Bamboo rolling mat (*makisu*)
- Nonstick gloves, optional (see page 95)
- Small bowl with ice water (see Tips, page 192)
- Wet towel
- *Yanagiba*, slicing knife or chef's knife (see Slicing Rolls, page 192)

TIPS

Any type of straight cucumber will work. We prefer to use Japanese cucumbers, since they are less seedy and as a result will be less watery, but English or Persian cucumbers will work too. If you are using English or Persian cucumbers, peel them and remove the seeds before using. Then cut the cucumber into 3½-inch (8.5 cm) lengths and then into thin sticks.

If you have a *katsuramuki* machine (turning slicer), you can use it to slice the cucumbers in this recipe (see page 46).

½	sheet nori (7 by 4 inches/17.5 by 10 cm; see page 195)	½
⅓ cup	Sushi Rice (page 143)	75 mL
Dab	wasabi paste	Dab
	Toasted sesame seeds (preferably a mix of black and white)	
2	pieces Japanese cucumber (*kyūri*), cut into sticks 3½ by ¼ by ¼ inch (8.5 by 0.5 by 0.5 cm; see Tips, left)	2
	Pickled ginger (*Gari*; page 27)	
	Wasabi paste	
	Soy sauce	

The Japanese word for cucumber is kyūri, *not* kappa. Kappa *are Japanese water spirits said to be fond of cucumbers, hence the name* kappamaki.

▲ Place nori on mat, shiny side down, with the longer side facing you.

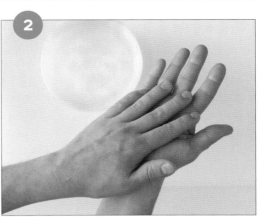

▲ Lightly wet your hands in the ice water, shaking or clapping off any excess (see Tips, page 200).

▲ Leaving a ½-inch (1 cm) border at the top of the nori, place rice on sheet, right of center.

▲ Using your fingers and pressing down and toward the right, spread rice to about 1 inch (2.5 cm) wide. Repeat Step 2.

▲ Using the tips of your fingers, continue to spread rice evenly over nori so remainder of nori is covered with rice, leaving ¼ inch (0.5 cm) visible at the top.

▲ Using your index finger, spread wasabi across center of rice.

▲ Lightly sprinkle sesame seeds over wasabi.

▲ Lay cucumber sticks evenly over wasabi and sesame.

▲ Place your thumbs under the bottom of the mat (the edge closest to you).

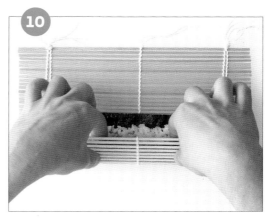

▲ Using your index fingers to hold the cucumber in place and rolling away from you, roll nori over cucumber, using your thumbs to lift the mat.

▲ With your hands cupped over the mat, gently squeeze mat on either side to begin to form the roll.

▲ Keeping pressure on the mat to shape the roll, continue to roll away from you until you reach the end of the mat.

▲ Using your middle and index fingers, gently tap on each end of the roll to ensure ingredients have not slipped out and are flush with nori.

TIPS

When making *maki*, you will need to rewet your hands repeatedly to prevent sticking. After wetting your hands, clap your hands together to remove excess water. (This will help to keep the nori dry.) Or you can use nonstick gloves (see page 95).

Once you begin rolling, it's important to lift the mat and roll in one fluid motion so the ingredients don't fall out (Steps 10 to 12).

▲ Lift off mat and place roll seam side down.

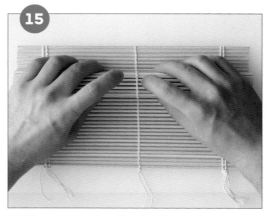

▲ Place mat over the roll and, with your thumbs on the side toward you, pinkies on the far side and other fingers cupped over the top, give the roll a light squeeze.

▲ Remove mat and slice roll (see page 192). If you prefer, cut the roll into 8 pieces.

▲ Arrange cut pieces upright on a serving plate. Garnish with additional wasabi, ginger and a small dipping bowl of soy sauce.

Tuna Roll *Tekkamaki*

Tekkamaki are traditional small rolls that are typically about 1 inch (2.5 cm) in diameter. You can use this technique to make small rolls containing many other ingredients (see Variations, below). Small rolls are usually accompanied by pickled ginger and additional wasabi, plus soy sauce for dipping.

MAKES 1 ROLL (6 PIECES)

EQUIPMENT

- Bamboo rolling mat (*makisu*)
- Wet towel
- Nonstick gloves, optional (see page 95)
- Small bowl with ice water (see Tips, page 206)
- *Yanagiba*, slicing knife or chef's knife (see Slicing Rolls, page 192)

TIP

You can purchase pickled ginger in well-stocked supermarkets or you can make your own (see page 27).

Tekka *translates to "red-hot iron," the color of the tuna, although some people believe it refers to* tekkaba, *the gambling rooms where this handheld snack was originally popular.*

½	sheet nori (7 by 4 inches/17.5 by 10 cm; see page 195)	½
⅓ cup	Sushi Rice (page 143)	75 mL
Dab	wasabi paste	Dab
2	strips tuna, cut into pieces each about 3¼ by ½ by ½ inch (8 by 1 by 1 cm)	2
	Pickled ginger (*Gari*; page 27)	
	Wasabi paste	
	Soy sauce	

VARIATIONS

Small rolls (*hosomaki*) are the most traditional rolls of Japan, and there are many variations. As a guideline, they should have no more than two ingredients, and the finished product should be about 1 inch (2.5 cm) in diameter.

Substitute salmon, eel or yellowtail for the tuna. Add a bit of sliced green onion or cucumber for a classic combination.

Vegetables in their pickled, cooked or raw state make an excellent small roll. They can be substituted for the fish. Cucumber is the most common raw vegetable used, but sliced avocado, thinly sliced carrot or green onions also work well. Pickled vegetables, including daikon, carrots and gourd (*kanpyō*), are also used, in combination with fish or by themselves (when using pickled vegetables, omit the wasabi inside the roll). Cooked vegetables such as asparagus, mushrooms and carrots can also be used, again omitting the wasabi.

A favorite combination is pickled plum paste (*umeboshi*), shiso (see page 26) and cucumber. In this recipe, substitute plum paste for the wasabi, then lay 3 to 4 shiso leaves on top and finish with sticks of cucumber.

▲ Place nori on mat, shiny side down, with the longer side facing you.

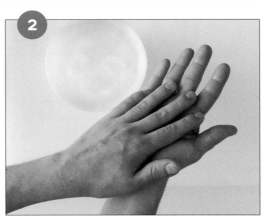

▲ Lightly wet your hands in the ice water, shaking or clapping off any excess (see Tips, page 206).

▲ Leaving a ½-inch (1 cm) border at the top of the nori, place rice on sheet, right of center.

▲ Using your fingers and pressing down and toward the right, spread rice to about 1 inch (2.5 cm) wide. Repeat Step 2.

▲ Using the tips of your fingers, continue to spread rice evenly over nori so remainder of nori is covered with rice, leaving ¼ inch (0.5 cm) visible at the top.

▲ Using your index finger, spread wasabi across center of rice.

▲ Lay sliced tuna evenly over wasabi.

▲ Place your thumbs under the bottom of the mat (the edge closest to you).

▲ Using your index fingers to hold the tuna in place and rolling away from you, roll nori over tuna, using your thumbs to lift the mat (see Tips, page 206).

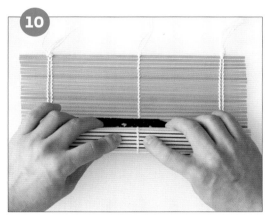

▲ With your hands cupped over the mat, gently squeeze mat on either side to begin to form the roll.

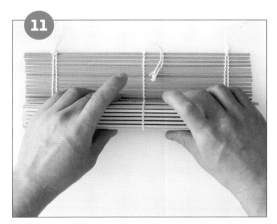

▲ Keeping pressure on the mat to shape the roll, continue to roll away from you until you reach the end of the mat.

▲ Using your middle and index fingers, gently tap on each end of the roll to ensure that ingredients have not slipped out and are flush with nori.

13

▲ Lift off mat and place roll seam side down.

14

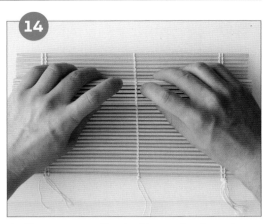

▲ Place mat over roll and, with your thumbs on the side toward you, pinkies on the far side and other fingers cupped over the top, give the roll a light squeeze.

15

▲ Remove mat and slice roll (see page 192). If you prefer, cut the roll into 8 pieces.

16

▲ Arrange cut pieces upright on a serving plate. Garnish with additional wasabi, ginger and a small dipping bowl of soy sauce.

TIPS

Some people add the vinegar from pickled ginger to the ice water used for wetting their hands and knife, to help prevent bacterial growth.

You will need to rewet your hands repeatedly throughout the process to prevent sticking. If you prefer, use nonstick gloves (see page 95).

After wetting your hands, clap them together to remove excess water (this will help to keep the nori dry).

After every cut, wipe clean and rewet your knife to prevent sticking and catching.

Inside-Out Rolls (*Uramaki*)

THE CALIFORNIA ROLL is where the inside-out roll began. It was created in Los Angeles in the early 1960s as a substitute for fatty tuna rolls, since at that time fatty tuna was hard to come by in the United States. Avocado was substituted for the fatty tuna and crab was added for a fishy flavor. Later it was turned inside out to hide the nori from American diners, who were unaccustomed to eating seaweed.

The spread in popularity of the California roll marked the beginning of an era of creativity among North American sushi chefs. This release from the rigid stricture of traditional rolls allowed chefs to experiment with ingredients and flavor combinations that would never have been allowed in a sushi restaurant in Japan.

Many of these new rolls were based on regional tastes, such as the Philadelphia roll, which contains smoked salmon, cucumber and cream cheese, and the Alaska Roll, which is a California roll made with salmon instead of crab.

There are two ways to make inside-out rolls (*uramaki*): using a bamboo mat for rolling, which is traditional, or using your hands to roll and then a bamboo mat to shape. Inside-out rolls are a bit easier to make than rolls with the nori outside (*norimaki*), because the rice helps the roll stick together. Another advantage is that inside-out rolls can be prepared in advance, as it is less important for the nori to be crisp. (If you are making rolls ahead of time, wrap them in plastic wrap to keep them crisp.)

California Roll *California-maki*

If North America's love of sushi could be traced back to one event, it would be the creation of the California roll (see page 209). The California roll conquered the United States and then the rest of the world, finally making its way back to Japan. While the original roll contained fake crab, this updated roll features the real thing.

MAKES 1 ROLL (6 PIECES)

EQUIPMENT

- Bamboo rolling mat (*makisu*), covered in plastic wrap (see Tips, below)
- Wet towel
- Nonstick gloves, optional (see page 95)
- Small bowl with ice water (see Tips, page 192)
- *Yanagiba*, slicing knife or chef's knife (see Slicing Rolls, page 192)

TIPS

After every cut, wipe clean and rewet your knife to prevent sticking and catching.

When making inside-out rolls, cover your mat in plastic wrap to avoid sticking and aid cleanup.

As an alternative to rolling with a mat, you can simply use your dampened hands to form the roll and then use a mat to tighten and shape the roll afterwards (see free-rolling technique, pages 219 to 220).

To apply fish roe to the outside of the roll, use your fingers or spread roe evenly on a plate and gently roll sushi in it until evenly covered.

1/2	sheet nori (7 by 4 inches/17.5 by 10 cm; see page 195)	1/2
1/3 cup	Sushi Rice (page 143)	75 mL
	Toasted sesame seeds (preferably a mix of black and white)	
2 oz	king crab leg meat	60 g
2	pieces Japanese cucumber (*kyūri*), each 3 1/2 by 1/4 by 1/4 inch (8.5 by 0.5 by 0.5 cm; see Tips, page 197)	2
1/8	avocado, sliced lengthwise	1/8
1/2 tsp	flying fish roe (*tobiko*), or to taste (optional, see Variations, below))	2 mL
	Pickled ginger (*Gari*; page 27)	
	Wasabi paste	
	Soy sauce	

VARIATIONS

You can use any type of crab you like: fresh or canned snow crab, king crab, lump crab meat, Jonah or Dungeness crab or fake crab sticks (*kani kama*).

If using fish roe, spread an even amount across the center of the nori (at end of Step 9, page 213) Alternatively, you can spread it on the outside of the finished roll, over the rice, before slicing (see Tips, left).

For a vegan version: Substitute vegan imitation crab.

For added flavor and to help hold the crab together, you can combine the shredded crab with Kewpie mayonnaise (Japanese-style mayo).

In some countries, such as the Philippines, mango is substituted for the avocado.

▲ Place nori on mat, shiny side down, with the longer side facing you.

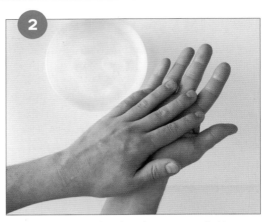

▲ Lightly wet your hands in the ice water, shaking or clapping off any excess (see Tips, page 206).

▲ Leaving a ½-inch (1 cm) border at the top of the nori, place rice on sheet, right of center.

▲ Using your fingers and pressing down and toward the right, spread rice to about 1 inch (2.5 cm) wide. Repeat Step 2.

▲ Using the tips of your fingers, continue to spread rice evenly over nori so remainder of nori is covered with rice, leaving ½ inch (0.5 cm) visible at the bottom.

▲ Sprinkle sesame seeds evenly over surface of rice.

▲ Flip nori over, rice side down, placing the bare edge closest to you.

▲ Lay crabmeat in a straight line across center of nori.

▲ On either side of crab, arrange an even line of cucumber and avocado, one on each side of the crab.

▲ Place your thumbs under the bottom of the mat (the edge closest to you; see Tips, page 211).

▲ Using your index fingers to hold the crab, avocado and cucumber in place, and rolling away from you, roll nori over fillings, using your thumbs to lift the mat.

▲ With your hands cupped over the mat, gently squeeze mat on either side to begin to form the roll.

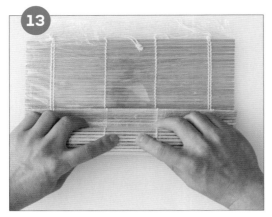

▲ Keeping pressure on the mat to shape the roll, continue to roll away from you until you reach the end of the mat.

▲ Using your fingers, gently tap on each end of the roll to ensure that ingredients have not slipped out and are flush with nori.

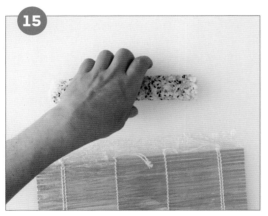

▲ Lift off mat and place roll seam side down on cutting board.

▲ Place mat over roll and, with your thumbs closest toward you, squeeze the roll lightly to form a squared cylinder.

▲ Remove mat and slice roll (see page 192).

▲ Arrange cut pieces upright on a serving plate. Garnish with wasabi, ginger and a small dipping bowl of soy sauce.

Spicy Tuna Roll

The California roll may have been the first inside-out roll, but the spicy tuna roll is quickly becoming the most popular. The combination of tuna and mayonnaise is a classic in Western culture, which may help to explain the appeal of this chile-spiked version of *uramaki* (inside-out roll). In this recipe we demonstrate forming the roll without the use of a mat (free rolling).

MAKES 1 ROLL (6 PIECES)

EQUIPMENT

- Wet towel
- Nonstick gloves, optional (see page 95)
- Small bowl with ice water (see Tips, page 192)
- Bamboo rolling mat (*makisu*), covered in plastic wrap (see Tips, below)
- *Yanagiba*, slicing knife or chef's knife (see Slicing Rolls, page 192)

TIPS

When making inside-out rolls, cover your mat in plastic wrap to avoid sticking and aid cleanup.

When rolling (Step 14), use your middle and index fingers to tap gently on the ends of the roll to ensure that ingredients have not slipped out and are flush with the nori.

$\frac{1}{2}$	sheet nori (7 by 4 inches/17.5 by 10 cm; see page 195)	$\frac{1}{2}$
$\frac{1}{3}$ cup	Sushi Rice (page 143)	75 mL
	Toasted sesame seeds (preferably a mix of black and white)	
1 tsp	Spicy Mayo (page 31)	5 mL
$1\frac{1}{2}$ tsp	thinly sliced green onion, white and green parts	7 mL
2	strips tuna, cut into pieces each about $3\frac{1}{4}$ by $\frac{1}{2}$ by $\frac{1}{2}$ inch (8 x 1 x 1 cm; about 2 oz/60 g)	2
	Pickled ginger (*Gari*; page 27)	
	Wasabi paste	
	Soy sauce	

VARIATIONS

You can substitute salmon, yellowtail, scallops or white fish for the tuna.

If you prefer, you can chop up the fish or cut into cubes and combine it with the spicy mayonnaise.

If desired, you can add 2 pieces of cucumber, cut into sticks $3\frac{1}{2}$ by $\frac{1}{4}$ by $\frac{1}{4}$ inch (8.5 by 0.5 by 0.5 cm), or $\frac{1}{4}$ avocado, sliced, to the filling. If so, you will need to reduce the amount of tuna to $1\frac{1}{2}$ oz (45 g) so the roll will close.

You can also add $\frac{1}{2}$ tsp (2 mL) flying fish roe (*tobiko*), either as a filling or spread over the outside of the roll before slicing.

▲ Place nori on board, shiny side down, with the longer side facing you.

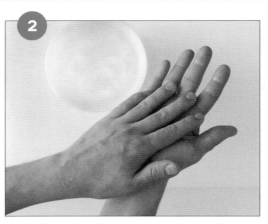

▲ Lightly wet your hands in the ice water, shaking or clapping off any excess (see Tips, page 206).

▲ Leaving a ¹/₂-inch (1 cm) border at the top of the nori, place rice on sheet, right of center.

▲ Using your fingers and pressing down and toward the right, spread rice to about 1 inch (2.5 cm) wide. Repeat Step 2.

▲ Using the tips of your fingers, continue to spread rice evenly over nori so remainder of nori is covered with rice, leaving ¹/₂ inch (0.5 cm) visible at the bottom.

▲ Sprinkle sesame seeds evenly over surface of rice.

▲ Flip nori over, rice side down, placing the uncovered edge toward you.

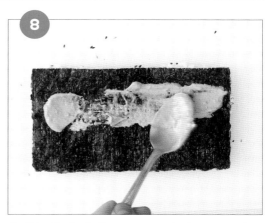

▲ Using the back of a spoon, spread spicy mayonnaise across center of nori.

▲ Sprinkle mayonnaise evenly with green onion.

▲ Lay sliced tuna evenly over onion. Place your thumbs under the bottom of the nori (the edge closest to you).

▲ Using your fingers to hold the fillings in place and rolling away from you, roll nori over fillings.

▲ With your hands cupped over the roll, gently squeeze on either side to begin to form the roll.

▲ Keeping pressure on the roll, continue to roll away from you until roll is sealed.

▲ Using your middle and index fingers, gently tap on each end of the roll to ensure that ingredients have not slipped out and are flush with the nori.

▲ Confirm roll seam side down (this will help ensure that the roll will not burst open when handled).

▲ Place mat over roll.

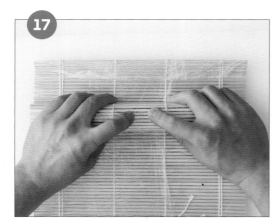

▲ With your thumbs on the side toward you, pinkies on the far side and other fingers cupped over the top, give the roll a light squeeze, forming a squared cylinder.

TIP

When making inside-out rolls, cover your mat in plastic wrap to avoid sticking and aid cleanup.

18

▲ Remove mat and slice roll (see page 192).

19

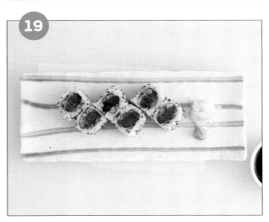

▲ Arrange cut pieces upright on a serving plate. Garnish with wasabi, ginger and a small dipping bowl of soy sauce.

Tempura Shrimp

Tempura is a frying method for seafood or vegetables that uses a light batter. It makes a great appetizer or light meal. In this recipe we fry shrimp in the crispy coating, but many other ingredients can be cooked this way. The next two rolls require you to prepare the main ingredient tempura-style in advance.

MAKES
6 TEMPURA
SHRIMP

EQUIPMENT

- Deep skillet or deep-fryer
- Deep-fry thermometer (see Tips, page 225)
- Chopsticks (see Tips, page 227)
- Spider (see Tips, page 225) or fine-mesh sieve
- Wire rack, placed on a baking sheet

TIP

You can find tempura shrimp at Asian markets. Some are already battered and ready to deep-fry. You can also find packaged tempura mix, to which you simply add an egg and water.

	Oil (vegetable or peanut), for frying	
2 cups	flour, for dusting	500 mL
1	batch Tempura Batter (page 227)	1
6	shrimp, prepared for tempura (see page 79)	6

VARIATIONS

Soft-Shell Crab Tempura: To make soft-shell crab tempura, follow the same steps but increase the cooking time by 2 to 3 minutes. One crab will make 1 or 2 rolls depending on your preference.

Vegetable Tempura: You can fry almost any vegetable in tempura batter. Try green onions, shiitake mushrooms, broccoli, onions, bell peppers or blanched green beans and carrots, or any of your favorite vegetables.

▲ Prepare tempura batter (see page 227).

▲ In deep skillet, heat 2 inches (5 cm) oil to 350°F (180°C). If you are using a deep-fryer, follow the manufacturer's instructions.

▲ Meanwhile, place flour in a shallow bowl.

▲ Working with 1 shrimp at a time, hold shrimp by the tail and lightly dip into flour, ensuring that it is completely covered. Shake off excess.

▲ Holding floured shrimp by the tail, dip into tempura batter, lightly coating all sides.

▲ Carefully dip battered shrimp into hot oil.

▲ Without letting go, swirl shrimp a few times in hot oil, then release into oil. Repeat with remaining shrimp, adding to hot oil one at a time.

▲ Once a shrimp has floated to the surface, cook for 1 minute, until crispy. If necessary, use chopsticks to turn shrimp while cooking.

▲ Using chopsticks or spider, remove shrimp from oil and transfer to wire rack until ready to use.

TIPS

If you are not using a deep-fryer, use a deep-fry thermometer to ensure that the oil remains at a constant 350°F (180°C) temperature.

Skim the oil regularly, using a spider (see below) to remove any bits of tempura and keep it clean.

A spider is a type of metal strainer with a wide, shallow mesh web at the end of a long handle. It is used for removing food from hot liquids and can be found in most kitchen supply stores.

Tempura Batter

Tempura batter should be made as close to use as possible, and in small batches. One of the keys to a good tempura batter is that it be very cold, so prepare it in a bowl set inside a larger bowl of ice to keep the batter chilled. You can find tempura flour (*tenpura ko*) at most Asian markets, but you can substitute all-purpose flour if needed.

MAKES ABOUT 2 CUPS (500 ML)

EQUIPMENT

- Mixing bowl
- Larger mixing bowl filled with ice (optional)
- Chopsticks (*hashi*)

TIPS

Use chopsticks to stir the batter, not a whisk, as you want a lumpy batter. Overmixing will result in a heavy batter that will absorb too much oil.

Some chefs use sparkling water for added lightness.

If you prefer a heavier batter, use less water; if you prefer a lighter batter, use more water. Experiment with the amount to see what you prefer.

If you are using all-purpose flour, add 1 tsp (5 mL) baking soda or baking powder.

Use the batter right away or keep cold until use. this makes more batter than you need for Tempura Shrimp.

1	large egg	1
1 cup	cold water, still or sparkling	250 mL
1 cup	tempura flour (*tenpura ko*) or all-purpose flour (see Tips, left)	250 mL

1. In bowl placed inside larger bowl filled with ice (if using), lightly beat egg.
2. Add water and whisk to combine.
3. Add flour and, using chopsticks, stir until just combined (batter will be very lumpy; see Tips, left). Use immediately.

VARIATION

To make a vegan batter suitable for use with vegetables, omit the egg. Combine equal parts all-purpose flour and ice-cold water to make a light batter. The finished fried product will be lighter in color than tempura made with egg.

Some chefs toss batter into the hot oil with their fingertips to create crispy bits, which they collect and adhere to whatever they are frying, for added volume and texture. You can also use them as a filling for rolls for added texture.

Shrimp Tempura Roll

Shrimp tempura rolls have a great combination of flavors and textures. They also make for a stunning presentation with the asparagus and shrimp tails sticking out of the ends of the roll.

MAKES 1 ROLL (6 PIECES)

EQUIPMENT

- Bamboo rolling mat (*makisu*), covered in plastic wrap
- Wet towel
- Nonstick gloves, optional (see page 95)
- Small bowl with ice water (see Tips, page 206)
- *Yanagiba*, slicing knife or chef's knife (see Slicing Rolls, page 192)

TIPS

Make and use the tempura shrimp as close as possible to when you are making the roll. Serve immediately so the shrimp remains crispy.

To cook the asparagus for this recipe, add to a skillet of boiling salted water and cook until al dente, about 2 minutes. Transfer to a bowl of ice water to stop the cooking, then pat dry with a paper towel.

½	sheet nori (7 by 4 inches/17.5 by 10 cm; see page 195)	½
⅓ cup	Sushi Rice (page 143)	75 mL
	Toasted sesame seeds (preferably a mix of black and white)	
1 tsp	Spicy Mayo (page 31)	5 mL
4	asparagus spears, cooked tender-crisp (see Tips, left)	4
2	pieces Tempura Shrimp (page 223)	2
	Pickled ginger (*Gari*; page 27)	
	Wasabi paste	
	Soy sauce	

VARIATIONS

You can add fillings such as a leaf of romaine lettuce heart, chopped green onion, sliced bell pepper, sliced red onion or sliced avocado, Kewpie mayonnaise (see page 31) or sweet chili sauce. Note that the more fillings you use, the thicker your roll will be and you may need to change the orientation of the nori to a vertical position (see pages 236 and 237).

For a vegetarian version: Omit the shrimp and double the amount of asparagus, frying one or more of the spears tempura-style. If desired, you can also use vegan imitation shrimp.

▲ Place nori on mat, shiny side down, with the longer side facing you.

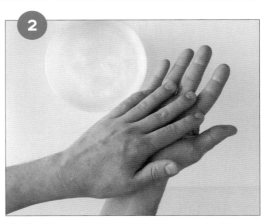

▲ Lightly wet your hands in the ice water; shaking or clapping off any excess (see Tips, page 206).

▲ Leaving a ¹/₂-inch (1 cm) border at the top of the nori, place rice on sheet, right of center.

▲ Using your fingers and pressing down and toward the right, spread rice to about 1 inch (2.5 cm) wide. Repeat Step 2.

▲ Using the tips of your fingers, continue to spread rice evenly over nori so remainder of nori is covered with rice, leaving ¹/₄ inch (0.5 cm) visible at the bottom.

▲ Sprinkle sesame seeds evenly over surface of rice.

▲ Flip nori over, rice side down, placing the bare edge toward you.

▲ Using the back of a spoon, spread spicy mayonnaise across center of nori.

▲ Place 2 pieces of asparagus on left and right ends of nori so tips stick out past the edges and ends butt against each other. Place remaining piece in the middle.

▲ Arrange shrimp tempura on top, with tails sticking out past both ends of nori.

▲ Place your thumbs under the bottom of the mat (the edge closest to you).

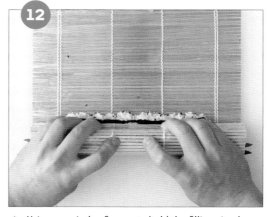

▲ Using your index fingers to hold the fillings in place and rolling away from you, roll nori over fillings, using your thumbs to lift the mat.

▲ With your hands cupped over the mat, gently squeeze mat on either side to begin to form the roll.

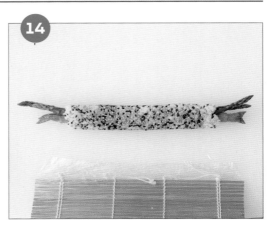

▲ Lift off mat and place roll seam side down.

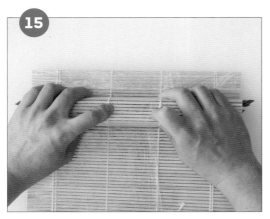

▲ Place mat over the roll and, with your thumbs on the side toward you, give roll a light squeeze to form a squared cylinder.

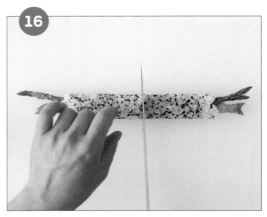

▲ Remove mat and slice roll (see page 192).

▲ Arrange cut pieces upright on a serving plate. Garnish with wasabi, ginger and a small dipping bowl of soy sauce.

ROLLING TIP

When rolling, maintain pressure on the mat to shape the roll and continue to roll away from you until you reach the end of the mat.

Spider Roll

In North America, soft-shell crabs are in season from around the beginning of May to September. After cleaning (see page 90), you will need to prepare and cook the crab tempura-style (see page 223). Many chefs cut the crab in half and make two rolls; we like to use one crab in each roll so that you get the whole crab, instead of one person getting the face and another the backside. Because the roll is so large, we rotate the nori to a vertical position after we spread the rice. This roll isn't as long as other rolls, so it's best to cut it into five pieces instead of six.

MAKES 1 ROLL (5 PIECES)

EQUIPMENT

- Bamboo rolling mat (*makisu*), covered in plastic wrap
- Wet towel
- Nonstick gloves, optional (see page 95)
- Small bowl with ice water (see Tips, page 206)
- *Yanagiba*, slicing knife or chef's knife (see Slicing Rolls, page 192)

TIP

To make two rolls instead of one, cut the crab in half lengthwise. You will need to double the amounts of remaining ingredients. After spreading the rice, you will also need to rotate the nori to a vertical position (see Step 7, page 237).

$\frac{1}{2}$	sheet nori (7 by 4 inches/17.5 by 10 cm; see page 195)	$\frac{1}{2}$
$\frac{1}{3}$ cup	Sushi Rice (page 143)	75 mL
	Toasted sesame seeds (preferably a mix of black and white)	
1 tsp	Spicy Mayo (page 31)	5 mL
$1\frac{1}{2}$ tbsp	thinly sliced green onion, white and green parts	22 mL
$1\frac{1}{2}$ tbsp	flying fish roe (*tobiko*)	22 mL
4	asparagus spears, cooked until crisp-tender (see Tips, page 229)	4
$\frac{1}{4}$	avocado, sliced lengthwise	$\frac{1}{4}$
1	soft-shell crab tempura (see page 223)	1
	Pickled ginger (*Gari*; page 27)	
	Wasabi paste	
	Soy sauce	

VARIATIONS

The addition of other vegetables works great in this roll, such as a leaf of romaine lettuce heart or a few slices of red onion. Reduce the amount of asparagus to 2 pieces if adding either of these.

Instead of spicy mayonnaise you can use plain mayo or tartar sauce for a more familiar flavor.

Soft-shell crabs are crabs that have recently molted, hence the new shells are still soft.

▲ Place nori on the cutting board, shiny side down, with the longer side facing you.

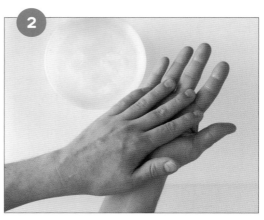

▲ Lightly wet your hands in the ice water, shaking or clapping off any excess (see Tips, page 206).

▲ Leaving a ½-inch (1 cm) border at the top of the nori, place rice on sheet, right of center.

▲ Using your fingers and pressing down and toward the right, spread rice to about 1 inch (2.5 cm) wide. Repeat Step 2.

▲ Continue to spread rice evenly so remainder of nori is covered with rice, leaving 1 inch (2.5 cm) of nori visible near your guide hand.

▲ Sprinkle sesame seeds evenly over surface of rice.

▲ Flip nori over, rice side down, placing uncovered edge at bottom of mat (nori should now be lengthwise).

▲ Using the back of a spoon, spread spicy mayonnaise across center of nori.

▲ Spread mayonnaise evenly with flying fish roe.

▲ Top with green onion.

▲ On either side of fish roe, place 2 pieces of asparagus so tips overhang edges of nori.

▲ Top with avocado.

▲ Center soft-shell crab on top of avocado, with legs extending past the sides.

▲ Place your thumbs under the bottom of the nori (the edge closest to you). Roll uncovered nori over crab, tucking it under the other side.

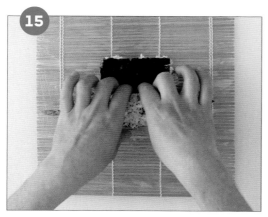

▲ Using your index fingers to hold the fillings in place and rolling away from you, roll nori over fillings. Keep pressure on the roll until it is sealed.

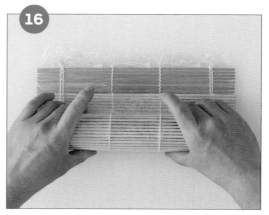

▲ Place roll seam side down on cutting board and place mat over the roll. Using your middle finger and thumb, gently press sides of roll.

▲ Remove mat and slice roll into 5 even pieces (see page 192).

▲ Place finished pieces upright on a serving plate. Garnish with wasabi, ginger and a small dipping bowl of soy sauce.

Dragon Roll

A dragon roll is so called because the top is covered in overlapping slices of avocado to resemble reptilian scales. There are several variations on this roll, but the most typical is an eel and cucumber roll covered with thin slices of avocado and topped with eel sauce or sweet, thickened soy.

MAKES 1 ROLL (8 PIECES)

EQUIPMENT

- Bamboo rolling mat (*makisu*), covered in plastic wrap
- Plastic wrap
- Wet towel
- Nonstick gloves, optional (see page 95)
- Small bowl with ice water (see Tips, page 206)
- *Yanagiba*, slicing knife or chef's knife (see Slicing Rolls, page 192)

TIPS

The eel may be warmed in a preheated 350°F (180°C) oven or toaster oven for a few minutes or until just heated through. Place eel skin side up on a foil-lined tray to prevent sticking.

To prepare the avocado for this recipe: Use a paring knife to remove the nib at the top. Insert the blade of the knife where the nib was and rotate the avocado from top to bottom to cut it in half lengthwise. Twist the two halves apart. With one motion, stick the knife into the pit and turn it 90 degrees, pulling out the pit as you twist the knife. Score the skin at the top of the avocado and peel off.

½	sheet nori (7 by 4 inches/17.5 by 10 cm; see page 195)	½
½ cup	Sushi Rice (page 143)	125 mL
1	7-inch (17.5 cm) piece eel (*unagi*), warmed in oven (see Tips, left)	
6	pieces Japanese cucumber (*kyūri*), cut into sticks 3½ by ¼ by ¼ inch (8.5 by 0.5 by 0.5 cm; see Tips, page 197)	6
½	avocado, pitted and peeled (see Tips, left)	½
1 tsp	Eel Sauce (page 19)	5 mL
	Toasted sesame seeds (preferably a mix of black and white)	
	Pickled ginger (*Gari*; page 27)	
	Wasabi paste	
	Soy sauce	

VARIATIONS

Using this technique, you can wrap almost any inside-out roll in avocado. Try adding avocado to a California roll, shrimp tempura roll or spider roll.

You can also put the avocado inside and the eel on top for something different.

Arranging the finished pieces in an S shape provides the perfect serpentine finishing touch.

▲ Place nori on mat, shiny side down, with the longer side facing you.

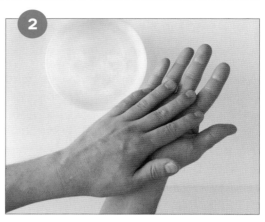

▲ Lightly wet your hands in the ice water, shaking or clapping off any excess (see Tips, page 206).

▲ Leaving a ½-inch (1 cm) border at the top of the nori, place rice on nori, right of center.

▲ Using your fingers and pressing down and toward the right, spread rice to about 1 inch (2.5 cm) wide. Repeat Step 2.

▲ Using the tips of your fingers, continue to spread rice evenly over nori so remainder of nori is covered with rice, leaving ¼ inch (0.5 cm) visible at the bottom.

▲ Flip nori over, rice side down, placing uncovered edge toward you.

▲ Lay eel evenly across center of nori. Arrange cucumber evenly on top of eel.

▲ Place your thumbs under the bottom of the nori (the edge closest to you).

▲ Using your fingers to hold the fillings in place and rolling away from you, roll nori over fillings.

▲ With your hands cupped over the roll, gently squeeze on either side and begin to shape the roll. Set roll aside.

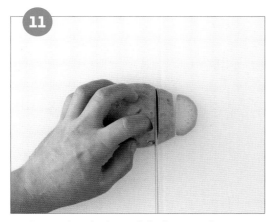

▲ Using a sharp knife, carefully slice avocado crosswise into pieces $\frac{1}{8}$ inch (3 mm) thick, leaving the slices in place.

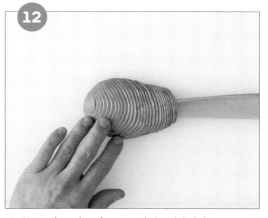

▲ Using the palm of your guide hand, lightly press down and forward on the avocado to fan it out.

▲ Gently slide the side of your knife under all the avocado slices at once, and then carefully transfer avocado to top of roll.

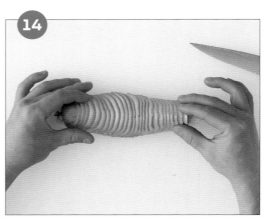

▲ Spread avocado over the length of the roll.

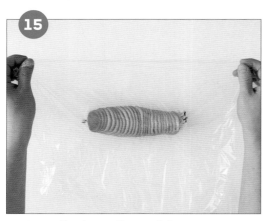

▲ Cover roll with a small piece of plastic wrap.

▲ Place mat on top of the roll and press down gently with your hands to wrap avocado around the roll. Remove mat, leaving plastic wrap in place.

▲ Following instructions on page 192, cut roll into 8 pieces, leaving plastic wrap on the roll as you cut.

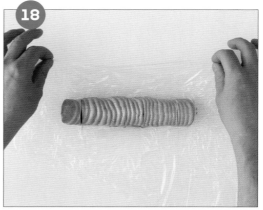

▲ Gently peel plastic wrap off each piece.

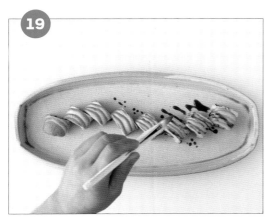

▲ Arrange pieces in an S shape on a serving plate. Drizzle eel sauce over roll and sprinkle with sesame seeds.

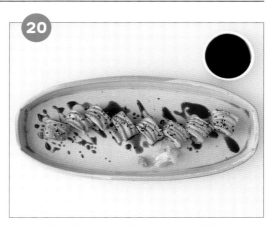

▲ Garnish with wasabi, ginger and a small dipping bowl of soy sauce. Serve immediately (remember, avocado oxidizes quickly).

Rainbow Roll

The rainbow roll is a California roll topped with assorted fish in different colors for a rainbow effect.

MAKES 1 ROLL (8 PIECES)

EQUIPMENT

- Bamboo rolling mat (*makisu*), covered in plastic wrap
- Plastic wrap
- Wet towel
- Nonstick gloves, optional (see page 95)
- Small bowl with ice water (see Tips, page 206)
- *Yanagiba*, slicing knife or chef's knife (see Slicing Rolls, page 192)

TIPS

If the roll becomes a little misshapen during slicing, just use your bamboo mat to reshape it.

Tuck overhanging fish into the ends of the roll. This will make it look cleaner and help the fish stick better to the ends of the roll.

Have all the ingredients prepared, including the sliced fish, before starting to assemble the roll.

Wiping the knife with a wet towel in between slices will result in cleaner cuts.

1	California Roll (page 211)	1
1	strip tuna (about 1 oz/500 g), sliced *sogizukuri*-style (see page 119)	1
1	strip yellowtail (about 1 oz/30 g), sliced *sogizukuri*-style	1
1	strip salmon (about 1 oz/30 g), sliced *sogizukuri*-style	1
1	strip white fish (fluke, snapper or striped bass; about 1 oz/30 g), sliced *sogizukuri*-style	1
1	piece sushi shrimp (*ebi*; see page 82)	1
¼	avocado, sliced lengthwise into 4 thin strips	¼
	Pickled ginger (*Gari*; page 27)	
	Wasabi paste	
	Soy sauce	

VARIATIONS

You can replace the California roll with any inside-out roll you prefer. Top it with the same "rainbow" selection of fish.

We like to make a similar-style roll with two types of tuna, for people who really love tuna. Take a spicy tuna roll (page 217) and top it with slices of tuna for a nice contrast of textures. If desired, drizzle the roll with additional spicy mayonnaise or your favorite hot sauce.

Arranging the cut roll in the shape of a rainbow enhances the effect.

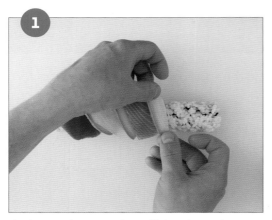

▲ Arrange alternating slices of fish and avocado at a slight angle on top of roll, following this order: tuna, white fish, salmon, yellowtail, ending with the shrimp.

▲ Cover top of rainbow roll with plastic wrap.

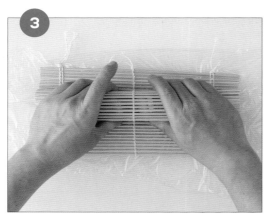

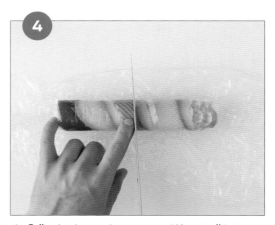

▲ Using your mat, gently press the avocado and fish onto the roll.

▲ Following instructions on page 192, cut roll into 8 pieces, leaving plastic wrap on the roll as you cut.

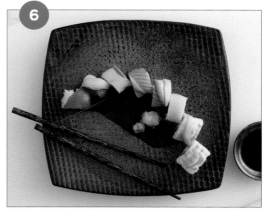

▲ Remove plastic wrap from each piece.

▲ Arrange pieces in an arc or rainbow shape on a serving plate. Garnish with wasabi, ginger and a small dipping bowl of soy sauce.

Large Rolls *Futomaki*

Large rolls allow you to put more ingredients inside them. Chefs try to create rolls that are both balanced in flavor and appealing to the eye. These large, thick-cut rolls use traditional ingredients for a variety of flavors, textures and colors. Don't limit yourself to the ingredients listed below. Try adding fresh seafood, grilled eel or fried tempura. Experiment with local, seasonal ingredients for an added twist on this classic roll. You can also omit the fish and load up on raw, cooked or pickled vegetables for a vegetarian version.

MAKES 1 ROLL (10 PIECES)

EQUIPMENT

- Bamboo rolling mat (*makisu*)
- Wet towel
- Nonstick gloves, optional (see page 95)
- Small bowl with ice water (see Tips, page 206)
- *Yanagiba*, slicing knife or chef's knife (see Slicing Rolls, page 192)

TIP

To make a half-roll, use a half-sheet of nori, rolled vertically, instead of a full sheet. Cut the roll into 5 or 6 pieces.

During Setsubun, the festival marking the day before the start of spring in Japan, it is traditional to serve futomaki *in their whole cylindrical form (i.e., uncut). We will cut ours, as that is how it is eaten the rest of the year.*

1	sheet nori (8 by 7 inches/20 by 17.5 cm)	1
1 cup	Sushi Rice (page 143)	250 mL
Dab	wasabi paste	Dab
	Toasted sesame seeds (preferably a mix of black and white)	
3 to 4	shiso leaves	3 to 4
3	pieces sushi shrimp (*ebi*; see page 82)	3
2	pieces Rolled Omelet (*Tamago*, page 32), cut into sticks $1/2$ by $1/2$ by $3^1/_2$ inches (1 by 1 by 8.5 cm)	2
1	strip tuna (about 1 oz/500 g), cut into pieces about $1/2$ by $3^1/_2$ inches (1 by 8.5 cm)	1
2	pieces Japanese cucumber (*kyūri*), cut into sticks $1/2$ by $3^1/_2$ inches (1 by 8.5 cm)	2
2 tbsp	*kanpyō* (pickled gourd strips; see page 36)	30 mL
	Pickled ginger (*Gari*; page 27)	
	Wasabi paste	
	Soy sauce	

VARIATIONS

We like to add 2 pieces of shrimp tempura and one 7-inch (17.5 cm) piece of grilled eel (*unagi*) for a crunchy texture and savory flavor.

To make a vegan version of this roll: Omit the fish. Add fresh lettuce leaves, asparagus, avocado, carrots and sprouts.

▲ Place nori on mat, shiny side down, with the shorter side facing you.

▲ Lightly wet your hands in the ice water, shaking or clapping off any excess (see Tips, page 206).

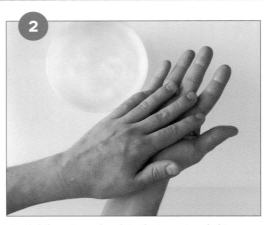

▲ Leaving a 2-inch (5 cm) border at the top of the nori, place rice on sheet, right of center.

▲ Using your fingers and pressing down and toward the right, spread rice to about 2 inches (5 cm) wide. Repeat Step 2.

▲ Using the tips of your fingers, continue to spread rice evenly over nori so all but the top 2 inches (5 cm) is covered with rice.

▲ Using your index finger, spread wasabi across center of rice.

▲ Sprinkle sesame seeds evenly over wasabi.

▲ Arrange 3 to 4 shiso leaves across center of rice.

▲ Place shrimp on top of shiso.

▲ Place *tamago* on top of shrimp. Place tuna on top of *tamago*.

▲ Arrange cucumber and *kanpyō* on either side of tuna.

▲ Place your thumbs under the bottom of the mat (the edge closest to you).

▲ Using your index fingers to hold the fillings in place and rolling away from you, roll nori over the filling, using your thumbs to lift the mat.

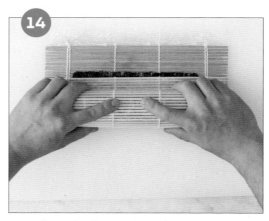

▲ With your hands cupped over the mat, gently squeeze mat on either side to begin to form the roll (see Tip, below).

▲ Keeping pressure on the mat to shape the roll, continue to roll away from you until you reach the end of the mat.

▲ Lift roll off mat and place seam side down on cutting board.

▲ Place mat over roll and, with your thumbs on the side toward you, pinkies on the far side and other fingers cupped over the top, give the roll a light squeeze.

ROLLING TIP

Using your middle and index fingers, gently tap on each end of the roll to ensure that ingredients have not slipped out and are flush with the nori.

▲ Cut roll in half, then cut each half into 5 even pieces.

▲ Arrange cut pieces upright on a serving plate. Garnish with additional wasabi, ginger and a small dipping bowl of soy sauce.

Teardrop-Shaped Roll

Teardrop-shaped rolls are a type of decorative roll (*kazaramaki*) that sushi chefs use to show off their skills. These rolls are very similar in preparation to small rolls (*hosomaki*), except they are shaped a bit differently. In addition to being served individually, if you treat each like a petal and place the narrow ends together, six teardrop rolls can be arranged to form a decorative flower-shape. These rolls are shaped like regular tuna rolls until you get to Step 9, at which point you pinch one side of the roll to form a teardrop shape.

MAKES 1 ROLL (6 PIECES)

EQUIPMENT

- Bamboo rolling mat (*makisu*)
- Wet towel
- Nonstick gloves, optional (see page 95)
- Small bowl with ice water (see Tips, page 206)
- *Yanagiba*, slicing knife or chef's knife (see Slicing Rolls, page 192)

TIPS

Instead of a teardrop shape, you can use the mat in Step 9 to shape this roll into a triangle: instead of rounding the back, you square it.

For a beautiful effect, you can also make three rolls with different fillings, arrange the rolls with the thick ends overlapping the thin ends, and then wrap them in a full sheet of nori (see photo, page 259).

½	sheet nori (7 by 4 inches/17.5 by 10 cm; see page 195)	½
⅓ cup	Sushi Rice (page 143)	75 mL
Dab	wasabi	Dab
2	strips tuna (about 1¼ oz/35 g), cut into piece each about 3¼ by ½ by ½ inch (8 by 1 by 1 cm)	2
	Wasabi paste	
	Pickled ginger (*Gari*; page 27)	
	Soy sauce	

VARIATIONS

Substitute an equal quantity of salmon, eel or yellowtail for the tuna. You can also add a little bit of sliced green onion or cucumber to any of these fish for a classic combination.

Vegetarian Teardrop Rolls: You can use any of the fillings you would use to make vegetarian small rolls: pickled vegetables (daikon, carrot or gourd/*kanpyō*), cooked vegetables (asparagus, mushrooms or carrot) or raw vegetables (cucumber, avocado, carrot or green onion). When using pickled or cooked vegetables, omit the wasabi inside the roll.

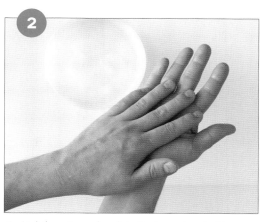

▲ Place nori on mat, shiny side down, with the longer side facing you.

▲ Lightly wet your hands in the ice water, shaking or clapping off any excess (see Tips, page 206).

▲ Leaving a ½-inch (1 cm) border at the top of the nori, place rice on sheet, right of center.

▲ Using your fingers and pressing down and toward the right, spread rice to about 1 inch (2.5 cm) wide. Repeat Step 2.

▲ Continue to spread rice evenly over nori so remainder of nori is covered with rice, leaving ¼ inch (0.5 cm) visible at the top and bottom.

▲ Using your index finger, spread wasabi across the rice about ½ inch (1 cm) down from top edge of rice.

▲ Lay sliced tuna evenly over wasabi.

▲ Lift the bottom of the mat and fold nori over the tuna, lining up the ends of the nori so the edges meet.

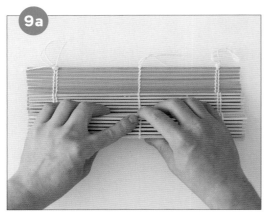

▲ Using the mat, press the roll into a teardrop shape.

▲ This sushi is not rolled but rather pressed into shape.

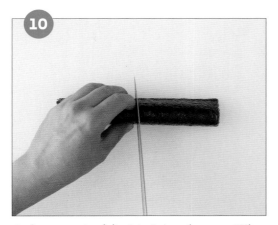

▲ Remove mat and slice into 6 pieces (see page 192).

▲ To serve, arrange the pieces in a circle with the thinner ends toward the center, so they resemble a flower. Garnish with additional wasabi, ginger and soy sauce.

Decorative Square Roll *Shikaimaki*

This is a show-stopping roll. It is fairly complex, a roll to make after you have mastered the other rolls in this book (call it your graduation roll). You start by making an intricate center. Then you roll a whole piece of cucumber in nori and quarter it. You then combine the two fillings to make the finished roll. The center will be a three-by-three cube of alternating tuna and *tamago*, creating a checkerboard of red and yellow, and the corners will be arches of green and white cucumber and rice.

MAKES 1 ROLL (6 PIECES)

EQUIPMENT

- Bamboo rolling mat (*makisu*)
- Wet towel
- Nonstick gloves, optional (see page 95)
- Small bowl with ice water (see Tips, page 206)
- *Yanagiba*, slicing knife or chef's knife (see Slicing Rolls, page 192)
- Offset spatula (optional)

TIPS

Use the straightest cucumber you can find for this recipe.

Do not peel the cucumber. If it is peeled, the nori will absorb the juice and become soggy and break.

Keep your work surface dry to prevent the nori from becoming soggy.

1	piece tuna, about 4 by $\frac{5}{8}$ by $\frac{1}{8}$ inch (10 cm by 1.5 cm by 3 mm)	1
1	piece Rolled Omelet (*Tamago*, page 32), about 4 by $\frac{1}{2}$ by $\frac{1}{8}$ inch (10 cm by 1 cm by 3 mm)	1
3	half-sheets nori (7 by 4 inches/ 17.5 by 10 cm; see page 195)	3
1	4-inch (10 cm) piece Japanese cucumber, unpeeled	1
$\frac{1}{2}$ cup	Sushi Rice (page 143)	125 mL

VARIATIONS

If you want to try something a little easier, you can use a single piece of tuna, salmon or rolled omelet (*tamago*) as the centerpiece of the roll, although it will be a little less decorative. You can also use about 2 oz (60 g) chopped crab.

Substitute an equal amount of salmon for the tuna and an equal amount of pickled daikon for the *tamago*.

This is the roll that sushi chefs pull out in competitions to really impress the judges!

TIP

The decorative center should be made a little ahead of time. Letting it rest at room temperature allows the pieces to adhere to each other, making it easier to prepare the roll.

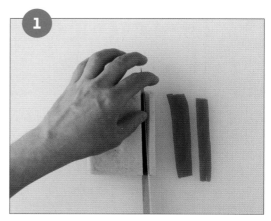

▲ Slice tuna and *tamago* into strips, each about ⅛ inch (3 mm) wide. You'll need 5 strips of tuna and 4 rectangular strips of *tamago*.

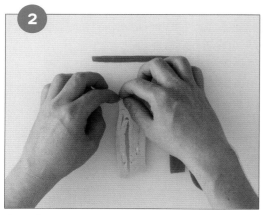

▲ Build the first layer: place 1 strip of tuna on cutting board.

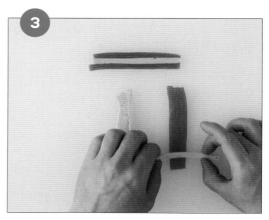

▲ Alongside tuna, place 1 strip of *tamago*, followed by another strip of tuna.

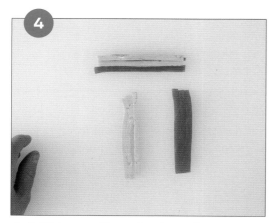

▲ Build the second layer: place 1 strip of *tamago* on top of first piece of tuna.

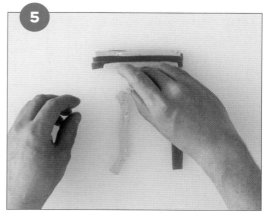

▲ Alongside *tamago*, place 1 strip of tuna, followed by another strip of *tamago*.

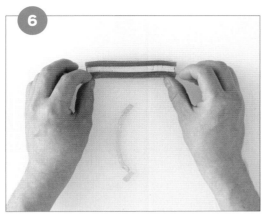

▲ Build the third layer: repeat Steps 2 and 3 on top of the second layer. Set aside.

▲ Place nori on mat, shiny side down, with the shorter side facing you.

▲ Place cucumber on nori at the edge closest to you.

▲ Place your thumbs under the bottom of the nori (the edge closest to you) and roll nori over cucumber until it is completely wrapped.

▲ When cucumber is wrapped in a single layer of nori, cut off excess nori. Set roll aside.

▲ Place another sheet of nori on mat, shiny side down, with the longer side facing you.

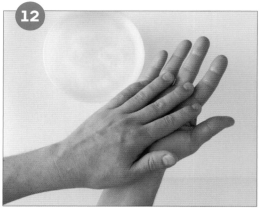

▲ Lightly wet your hands in the ice water, shaking or clapping off any excess (see Tips, page 206).

▲ Leaving a 1/2-inch (1 cm) border at the top of the nori, place rice on sheet, right of center.

▲ Spread rice, about 1 inch (2.5 cm) wide, leaving a 2-inch (5 cm) area uncovered at the side closest to your cutting hand.

▲ Rotate nori 90 degrees so uncovered area is positioned opposite you, at the top.

▲ Place nori-wrapped cucumber lengthwise in center of rice.

▲ Place your thumbs under the bottom of the mat (the edge closest to you).

▲ Using your index fingers to hold the cucumber in place and rolling away from you, roll nori over nori-wrapped cucumber, using your thumbs to lift the mat.

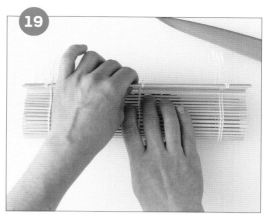

▲ Keeping pressure on the mat to shape the roll, continue to roll away from you until you reach the end of the mat.

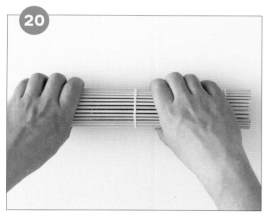

▲ With your hands cupped over the mat, gently squeeze on either side to begin to form the roll.

▲ Lift off mat and place roll seam side down on cutting board.

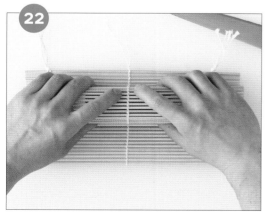

▲ Place mat over the roll and, with your thumbs on the side toward you, pinkies on the far side and other fingers spread over the top, give the roll a light squeeze.

▲ Remove mat (you should have a nice cylindrical roll). Rotate roll 90 degrees so that it is perpendicular to front of the board.

▲ Dip the tip of your knife in the ice water, then, in a swift motion, stand the knife up on the end of its handle so that the water drips down the edge of the knife.

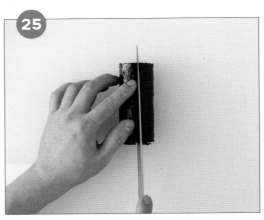

▲ Place your forefinger on the spine of the knife. Using a slight rocking motion, slice the roll in half lengthwise.

▲ Wipe your knife with the wet towel.

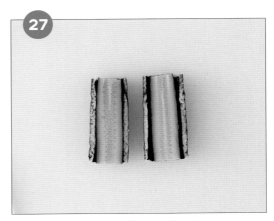

▲ Place the 2 pieces parallel to each other and perpendicular to front of the board.

▲ Repeat Steps 24 to 27, slicing the first piece in half lengthwise.

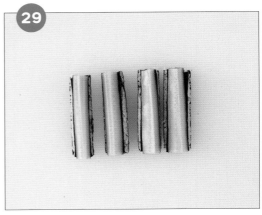

▲ Repeat Steps 24 to 27, slicing the second piece in half lengthwise. You should now have 4 lengthwise quarters of the cucumber roll.

▲ Place remaining sheet of nori on cutting board, with the short side facing you.

▲ Place 1 quarter cucumber roll on the center of the nori, with the cucumber facing toward you and the arch of nori away from you.

▲ Place another quarter cucumber roll directly behind the first, with nori facing you.

▲ Slide a knife under decorative center; turn it to make a diamond shape and place between two pieces of cucumber roll so its sides are resting on their backs.

▲ Place third quarter of cucumber roll on far side of decorative center, with nori resting on it and cucumber facing up to form a corner of the roll.

▲ Place last quarter of cucumber roll on near side of decorative center, with nori resting on it and cucumber facing up to form a corner of the roll.

▲ Place your thumbs under the bottom of the nori sheet (the edge closest to you).

▲ Using your index fingers to hold the fillings in place, wrap nori over fillings, pressing it onto rice.

▲ Continue to roll until seam is face down on cutting board (you are rolling decorative center over remaining nori to seal the roll).

▲ Place mat over the roll and press to square off perfectly.

▲ Remove mat and slice roll (see page 192).

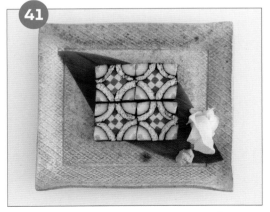

▲ Place finished pieces upright on a serving plate. Garnish with wasabi, ginger and a small dipping bowl of soy sauce.

Cucumber-Wrapped Roll

This roll contains no rice or seaweed—sheets of cucumber take the place of the traditional wrappings. It can be made a few hours ahead of time for a party. Before slicing, wrap in plastic wrap and refrigerate. Slice just before serving.

MAKES 1 ROLL (6 PIECES)

EQUIPMENT

- Bamboo rolling mat (*makisu*), covered in plastic wrap
- Wet towel
- Nonstick gloves, optional (see page 95)
- Small bowl with ice water (see Tips, page 206)
- Vegetable peeler (optional)
- *Yanagiba*, slicing knife or chef's knife (see Slicing Rolls, page 192)

TIPS

The cucumber is sliced using the *katsuramuki* technique, which may take practice. You can also use a vegetable peeler to create long strips of cucumber.

English cucumbers work best for this recipe. They are usually a bit larger and straighter than Japanese or Persian cucumbers.

Be sure to pat dry the cucumber strips (Step 2). Otherwise the moisture will encourage ingredients to slide out the sides of the roll. For the same reason, ensure that the roll is tight.

1	English cucumber, cut crosswise into 1 piece $4\frac{1}{2}$ inches (11 cm) long (see Tips, left)	1
2 oz	crabmeat, mixed with 1 tbsp (15 mL) mayo (just enough to bind)	60 g
2	slices avocado	2
	Pickled ginger (*Gari*; page 27)	
	Wasabi paste	
	Soy sauce	

VARIATIONS

Substitute an equal amount of daikon radish, sliced *katsuramuki*-style (page 24), for the cucumber. Rinse the sliced daikon under cold running water for 30 seconds to 1 minute to remove any strong radish flavor and odor. Rinsing will also help to crisp the radish. For added flavor, marinate daikon slices in pickling liquid (*amazu*, see page 37) and pat dry with paper towels before assembly.

Rolls using this technique can be filled with the same ingredients that you would use to make traditional rolls (*makizusihi*).

Vegan Cucumber-Wrapped Roll: Substitute 2 oz (60 g) julienned red bell pepper or vegan imitation crab for the crab meat.

▲ Prepare sheets of cucumber 12 inches (30 cm) long, following the *katsuramuki* technique on page 24. You'll want to use the whole cucumber, omitting the seeds.

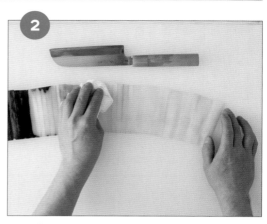

▲ Lightly pat dry a prepared cucumber sheet (see Tips, page 271).

▲ Lay cucumber lengthwise on your cutting board skin side down. Place crab and avocado side by side at bottom of cucumber (the section with the skin on it).

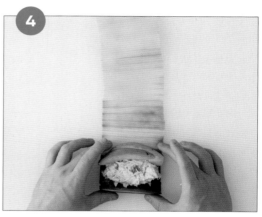

▲ Using your index fingers to hold the crab and avocado in place, and rolling away from you, roll cucumber over fillings, tucking in the end over the ingredients.

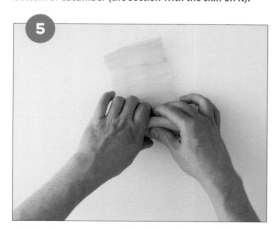

▲ Keeping pressure on the roll, continue to roll away from you until the roll is sealed.

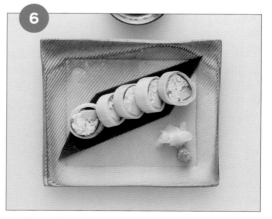

▲ Slice roll (see page 192). Place finished pieces upright on a serving plate. Garnish with wasabi, ginger and a small bowl of soy sauce for dipping.

Hand Rolls (*Temaki*)

HAND ROLLS (*temaki*) are time-honored rolls made with your hands and eaten with your hands. Traditionally hand rolls were served toward the end of a sushi meal. In higher-end sushi bars you would finish with a *toro* and green onion hand roll—the end of the meal being a time for the sushi chef to show off his or her prized tuna and best-quality nori. Nowadays hand rolls are eaten at any time during the meal, interspersed with cut rolls. They can be filled with any of the ingredients you find in cut rolls.

Hand rolls are a great dinner-party idea. Prepare the sushi rice and a wide array of fillings ahead of time and let your guests make their own rolls.

Toro Green Onion Hand Roll

Tuna and green onion is a classic combination. Using fatty tuna (*toro*) takes this roll to the next level, while the green onion adds both flavor and texture.

MAKES
1 HAND ROLL

TIPS

Make sure your hands are very dry before you begin rolling, so the nori remains crisp.

You want to roll the nori tightly enough to contain the fillings but not so tightly that it breaks.

Once you complete the roll, use a single grain of sushi rice on the inside corner of the nori to help seal the cone.

Serve hand rolls immediately after making so the nori doesn't get soggy.

½	sheet nori (7 by 4 inches/17.5 by 10 cm; see page 195)	½
¼ cup	Sushi Rice (page 143)	60 mL
Dab	wasabi paste	Dab
1	strip fatty tuna (*toro*; about 1 oz/30 g), finely chopped	1
1 tbsp	thinly sliced green onion, white and green parts	15 mL

VARIATIONS

Use your imagination: any ingredient that you would put in rolled sushi will work in a hand roll.

For a vegetarian version: Use raw or pickled vegetables. Try mixing and matching julienned cucumber or carrot, chopped green onion, shiitake and enoki mushrooms, asparagus, avocado, julienned bell pepper, romaine lettuce, radish sprouts—the choices are limitless.

▲ Place nori shiny side down in the palm of your dominant hand.

▲ Place rice on nori slightly to the right of center.

▲ Using the tips of your fingers, spread rice evenly over nori, stopping halfway across so half the sheet is covered with rice and half is not.

▲ Using your fingers, make a little indentation in the rice to place your ingredients.

▲ Using your index finger, dab a little wasabi in center of indentation.

▲ Arranging it parallel to short edge of nori, place tuna on top of rice.

▲ Scatter green onion on top of tuna.

▲ Lift the bottom left corner of nori up and over fillings. Roll toward the top corner of rice, wrapping rice and fillings tightly (see Tips, page 274).

▲ Continue rolling to form a cone shape (see Tips, page 274).

▲ Once cone is complete, serve immediately, with additional wasabi, ginger and a small dipping bowl of soy sauce.

CYLINDER-SHAPED HAND ROLL

Instead of rolling the nori into a cone, you can roll it into a cylinder. Simply follow Steps 1 to 8, but instead of rolling the nori across, keep the top and bottom edges aligned and roll straight into a cylinder.

Stuffed Sushi (*Inarizushi*)

TRADITIONALLY, STUFFED SUSHI (*inarizushi*) is a simpler type of sushi in which deep-fried thin tofu pouches (*abura-age*), steeped in seasonings such as dashi, sake, mirin, soy and sugar, are stuffed with sushi rice. This makes them a great option for vegetarians. In this chapter we also provide options for flavored fillings.

The prepared pouches (*inari*) are 2 by 4 inches (5 by 10 cm) and come pre-seasoned and packaged in cans or vacuum-sealed bags. To use, pat them dry and pull open one end (much like pita bread). They are now ready to stuff. If desired, you can also prepare *abura-age* for *inari* yourself (see page 279).

Because *inarizushi* are easily portable and can be stored in the refrigerator for up to a week, they make a great breakfast or midmorning snack and are a nice alternative for kids' school lunches.

How to Prepare Abura-age for *Inari*

Abura-age is tofu skin that has been deep-fried, creating a pocket that is ideal for stuffing. You can purchase prepared *inari* pouches from a Japanese grocer or you can make them at home from store-bought *abura-age*. It is easy to do. You first blanch the *abura-age* in boiling water and then squeeze out the water to remove some of the oiliness. Then you cook them again with seasonings.

MAKES 6 POUCHES

TIPS

The advantages to preparing your own *abura-age* are that the flavor and texture are superior and that you can adjust the seasonings to suit your taste.

Look for *abura-age* in the refrigerated or freezer section of a Japanese grocery store.

6	*abura-age* sheets, cut in half	6
1 cup	dashi (page 22)	250 mL
1/3 cup	granulated sugar	75 mL
3 tbsp	soy sauce	45 mL

1. Bring to a boil a medium saucepan of water. Add halved *abura-age* and return to a boil; simmer for 1 minute. Remove from heat and drain, discarding liquid. Set aside until cool enough to handle. Using your hands, squeeze out excess liquid.
2. In a clean saucepan, combine dashi, sugar and soy sauce and bring to a boil.
3. Add prepared *abura-age*. Reduce heat to low, cover and simmer for 15 minutes or until most of the liquid has been absorbed.
4. Set aside until cool enough to handle.
5. Using your hands, squeeze out any excess liquid. You can now use the *inari* for *inarizushi*. Refrigerate for up to 3 days or freeze for up to 1 month.

Believed to have been invented in the middle of the 19th century, inarizushi *gets its name from* Inari, *the Shinto* kami (spirit) *of rice, tea, sake and foxes—in Japanese myth, fried tofu is a favorite food of foxes. The points on the stuffed pouches resemble a fox's pointed ears.*

Shiso Ginger Stuffed Sushi *Inarizushi*

Stuffed sushi is known as *inarizushi*. This recipe is one we like to take on picnics. Other possible fillings include plain sushi rice, *furikake*-flavored sushi rice or finely diced cooked seasonal vegetables (whatever you have on hand in your fridge or garden) mixed with sushi rice.

MAKES 6 PIECES

TIPS

Chop the ginger very finely—into rice-size pieces—so that it blends into the rice.

Store *inarizushi* in an airtight container in the refrigerator for up to 1 week. Bring to room temperature before serving.

Look for soy-seasoned mushrooms (see Variations, right) in Japanese markets. To make your own, combine 1 cup (250 mL) dried shiitake mushrooms, $\frac{1}{3}$ cup (75 mL) water, 2 tbsp (30 mL) soy sauce and 1 heaping tsp (6 mL) granulated sugar in a small saucepan. Cover and bring to a boil; reduce heat to low and simmer until mushrooms are softened and all the liquid is absorbed, 12 to 15 minutes. This will make more than you need for one batch of *inarizushi*; refrigerate leftovers for up to 5 days.

1 cup	Sushi Rice (page 143)	250 mL
1 tbsp	pickled ginger (*Gari*; page 27), finely chopped (see Tips, left)	15 mL
$1\frac{1}{2}$ tsp	toasted sesame seeds (mix of black and white)	7 mL
2	shiso leaves, cut into fine shreds (chiffonade)	2
6	tofu pouches (*inari*; see page 279)	6
	Pickled ginger (*Gari*; page 27), for garnishing	

VARIATIONS

Furikake-*Flavored Sushi Rice:* Season the sushi rice to taste with *furikake*, a prepackaged rice seasoning that contains ground dried fish, sesame, seaweed and salt.

Mushroom and Carrot Inarizushi: To sushi rice, add 2 tbsp (30 mL) each finely diced soy-seasoned shiitake mushroom and carrot; stir to combine well. Soy-seasoned mushrooms can be found at Japanese markets.

Tamago and Green Onion Inarizushi: To sushi rice, add 3 tbsp (45 mL) diced *tamago* and 1 tbsp (15 mL) finely chopped green onion; stir to combine well.

Pickled Radish and Burdock Root Inarizushi: Reduce amount of sushi rice to $\frac{3}{4}$ cup (175 mL). Stir into rice 2 tbsp (30 mL) each finely diced pickled daikon radish (*takuan*) and burdock root (*gobō*).

▲ In a bowl, combine rice, ginger, sesame seeds and shiso. Stir to combine.

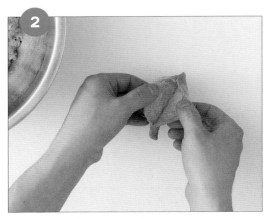

▲ Using your fingers, carefully tear open one end of a tofu pouch.

▲ Spoon filling into pouch until about half full.

▲ Gently pack down rice with your fingers (be careful not to pack too tightly or the pouch will break).

▲ Fold edges of pouch over rice to seal. Repeat with remaining pouches.

▲ Arrange pouches seam side down on a serving plate. Garnish with wasabi, additional ginger and a small dipping bowl of soy sauce.

Presentation

SUSHI IS OFTEN considered an art form, with the sushi chef being the artist. Each plate is different, whether it be a large sashimi arrangement, a plate of sushi or a mixed plate of sashimi, sushi and *maki*. Plates are arranged to entice diners visually before they eat, a practice called *moritsuke*. Each serving is expected to have a balance of colors, styles and space. Your first sense to experience food is sight: the colors and arrangement should make you want to eat the sushi.

When arranging sashimi, a chef once told me, think of mountains sloping down to the sea. Start with the larger, bold items in the back and work your way down to more subtle balancing items. If possible, arranging sashimi on a bed of ice is a great way to present the colors of the fish, and it will help keep the fish cold. When garnishing, slices of citrus (lime, lemon, *sudachi* or yuzu) will help accentuate the fish and make the colors on the plate really pop. Flowers or leaves from the garden will provide added contrast and really give the plate a personal feel.

When arranging sashimi and sushi, it is a good rule of thumb to stagger the different colors. You don't want to put all the bold colors on one side of the plate, as it will look heavier on that side and not balanced. It is best to arrange colors from bold to light to bold to light. For example, if you start with tuna sushi, you will want to follow with some type of white fish, and then continue to alternate the colors.

Creating a Sushi Plate

Sushi plates often contain one *maki* roll, a piece of *tamago* and seven or eight pieces of sushi. You should start by making the roll first and placing it at the back of the plate. The sushi is then arranged diagonally from the left-hand side of the plate to the right, as the majority of people will be reaching from the right. Cooked items that have a sauce, such as eel, are placed toward the front of the plate. Shrimp tails should face forward.

In most cases the pickled ginger and wasabi are placed on the right so they are easily noticeable. If you are arranging a larger plate of sushi for a party, multiple servings of ginger and wasabi can be added on both sides of the plate, or you can serve them on the side in individual dishes. Bamboo leaves (*sasa*) may be placed on the plate or between each row of *maki* and sushi. Note that when the plate is finished, there should be an equal amount of empty space around the edges.

For a plate of *makizushi*, the rolls can be arranged in slightly different ways for added appeal. The typical way to arrange a *maki* roll is on a slight diagonal, with each pair of slices slightly staggered. You can also place them in a straight line or an arc or stack them one on top of the other.

For a larger plate of mixed sushi, sashimi and *maki* rolls, follow the instructions given above and simply combine them. Start by placing the assorted rolls at the back of the plate, followed by *nigiri* sushi in the middle (you can separate them with bamboo leaves if you like). Keep any items such as eel separate so their sauce doesn't get on the other pieces of sushi. The sashimi is then placed toward the front of the plate, since it is usually eaten first.

Serving Plates

As for what types of plates to serve on, traditionally footed wooden boards are used. However, you can use whatever serving plates you like. We do recommend that they be all white or a single light color so they don't detract from the presentation of the sushi. Round platters work well for assortments for two or more people, as you can arrange the presentation to face in more than one direction.

Let your inner artist run free when plating. The broad palette of colors provided by the oceans allows you to be creative in your presentation. Remember, if it looks pleasing and appetizing to you, it will to your guests as well. *Itadakimasu* and *bon appétit*!

Glossary: Fish and Seafood for Sushi

THERE ARE MORE THAN 67,000 species of crustacean, 27,000 species of fish and 9,200 species of bivalve in the world's waters—and a multitude more remain unidentified. Not all fish or seafood makes great sushi, and not all migratory fish are best wherever and whenever you catch them. This chapter discusses those that are the most suited for use in sushi, as well as their sustainability and seasonality.

When possible, we also offer suggestions for substitutions.

The earth's oceans are vast, and although their bounty seems limitless, industrial-scale fishing practices—in place since the 1800s—have made it impossible for fish stocks to keep up. Making informed decisions when purchasing fish and seafood is imperative.

SAFETY GUIDELINES FOR EATING RAW FISH AND SEAFOOD

Raw fish and seafood can carry parasites, bacteria or algae (think oysters and red tide toxins); in addition, raw items can pick up bacteria during preparation, either from the cutting board or by cross-contamination from other ingredients. For these reasons, it is recommended that pregnant women, infants and young children, as well as elderly people—in other words, those whose immune system may not be fully developed or in its prime—avoid consuming raw fish or seafood.

In the United States, the law requires that all fish to be served raw are frozen for at least 15 hours at −31°F (−35°C) or 7 days at −4°F (−20°C) to kill parasites; tuna is the only fish that is exempt from freezing, as it isn't prone to parasites. (Canada has similar regulations.) Although this law isn't enforced and there is some confusion about who is responsible for enforcing it—the supplier or the restaurant—many restaurants take it upon themselves to freeze their fish, not just to remove the potential for parasites but also to increase year-round availability of certain types of fish on their menus. This type of freezing requires a commercial freezer; your home freezer does not freeze fast enough or get cold enough to kill parasites.

Fish that spend time in fresh water are especially prone to parasites. For this reason, when using freshwater fish for sushi, we recommend that you make sure it has been properly frozen first.

We do not wish to scare you away from raw fish or seafood, as the risks are minimal. As with everything, we just want you to make informed decisions.

BACTERIA-FIGHTING INGREDIENTS

The seasonings and garnishes that accompany sushi and sashimi do more than enhance flavor. Vinegar, the main seasoning in sushi rice, has excellent disinfecting and antibacterial properties. Pickled ginger is also antibacterial—the gingerroot itself as well as the vinegar used to pickle it. Freshly grated wasabi is also a strong bacteria fighter. The compound that gives wasabi its pungency, isothiocyanate, is believed to inhibit bacterial growth.

Here are some questions to ask your chef, grocer or fishmonger:

- Where is the fish from? Is it wild or farm-raised?
- How is it caught? Was it pole-caught, trawled or long-line caught? Is there a lot of bycatch?
- If farmed, how is it farmed? Open pens or closed tanks?

You can also simply ask which choices are sustainable. Even if your purveyor doesn't know the answers, asking questions lets him or her know that you are a concerned consumer. If enough people ask these questions, purveyors will question their suppliers.

Sustainability is a large, complex topic. We recommend that you consult reliable websites such as www.seafoodwatch.org or www.worldwildlife.org for the most current information before purchasing fish or seafood. There are also some apps for your phone (check out Seafood Watch) that you can use while shopping.

Seasonality is another factor to consider when buying fish and seafood. Many of our favorites are most plentiful, and flavorful, only during specific months of the year. For example, soft-shell crabs are in season from May to July, and Copper River salmon from Alaska are in season from mid-May to mid-June. Each year markets and restaurants celebrate their return. Buying seasonally promotes sustainability by supporting the fishers who are catching the fish and seafood at its peak.

See Fish and Seafood: Buying, Storing and Butchering (page 55) for best practices on the handling and storage of fish and seafood.

WHAT IS SUSHI-GRADE FISH?

"Sushi-grade fish" is a made-up marketing term. There are no rules, guidelines or definitions surrounding its use. In fact, many fishmongers will label fish "sushi grade" simply because it's the best fish they have on hand.

Fish

Amberjack (*Kanpachi*)

Similar in appearance to yellowtail (see page 292), amberjack has a yellow stripe running down the length of its body. Different species of amberjack exist all over the world; the species we are referring to is native to the Pacific Ocean, from Japan to Hawaii.

Amberjack is related to the yellowtail family but has a less fatty, lighter, simpler taste than its richer cousin yellowtail. Its flavor is also described as being a bit sweet,

making it an exceptional pairing with sushi rice. Because of its firm texture, amberjack is great for sashimi.

Interestingly, the names of amberjack change depending on its age. In the spring, the Japanese refer to the young fish as *shiokko*. In the early summer, it is referred to as *hiramasa* (flat amberjack). In its most mature stage, it is referred to as *kanpachi*. *Kanpachi* is at its peak in the late summer.

These days most amberjacks are farmed-raised, making them available year-round.

Substitutions: yellowtail, *shiokko* or *hiramasa* (readily available farmed from Australia); *kona kanpachi* (from Hawaii).

Eels

The Japanese have different names for fresh- and salt-water eels. Freshwater eels are referred to as *unagi*, while sea eels are *anago*. Freshwater eel is never eaten raw, but rather is served cooked and coated eel sauce in *nigiri*. Saltwater eel are eaten raw as sashimi, or lightly cooked to soften the bones for *nigiri*.

Because *unagi* is very difficult to prepare, it is generally bought precooked by *unagi* chefs. To prepare *unagi*, it is first grilled to

melt some of its fat, then it is steamed to make it fluffy, and then it is grilled again while being repeatedly basted with eel sauce (see page 19). The finished product is sweet and flaky. *Unagi* are available year-round from Japan but are considered best in the fall, when they move from rivers to the ocean to lay their eggs.

Anago can be eaten raw as sashimi with the bones still in, usually accompanied by grated ginger. It has a slippery texture and delicate taste. For *nigiri*, *anago* is lightly simmered to soften the bones and is typically served with just a little citrus zest (no soy sauce or wasabi is used). *Anago* is available year-round from Japan but is considered best in the winter and summer. In winter it is richer in texture and flavor; in summer it is lighter.

Fluke (*Hirame*)

Fluke is considered a flatfish; it is grouped in the same category as turbot, flounder and sole. In Japan it is called *hirame*, which literally translates to "flat fish."

Flatfish live on the bottom of the ocean; as a result, both of their eyes are on one side (the top) of their head, and the bottom of the fish is white because of lack of pigment. Depending on type, a flatfish's eyes will be located on either the right or left side. You can tell if you have a fluke or a flounder by which side the eyes are on when it is lying down on the white part. The Japanese have a saying for it: "*hidari hirame, migi karei*" (left, fluke; right, flounder).

The white flesh of the fluke should have a clean ocean flavor and meaty texture. Fluke is excellent for the sashimi preparation *usuzukuri*, in which the fish is sliced super-thin (page 123); it is also used for *nigiri* (page 147).

Flukes have an outer muscle called the *engawa*, which is considered a delicacy because one fish provides only four small pieces. The *engawa* have a very chewy, meaty texture.

Fluke is usually served with ponzu sauce (page 29), but it also pairs well with sea salt and slices of citrus, which draw out its natural flavors. To demonstrate its delicate taste, fluke is often the first piece of sushi served during a meal.

Along the east coast of the United States, fluke is in season during the summer. In Japan, it is in season during the fall and winter months. Farm-raised fluke from Korea is available year-round.

Flounder abound all over the world; their peak season in Japan is summer. Turbot is available both wild and farmed year-round; its peak season runs from April to June.

Substitutions: flounder (*karei*), turbot, sole, halibut (*hirame*).

Mackerel (*Saba*)

Mackerel is one of the most abundant and therefore sustainable ocean fish. It is also one of the healthiest to eat, because of its high levels of omega-3 fats. Its strong fishy taste makes it an unpopular choice among novice sushi eaters, but sushi aficionados tend to seek it out.

Mackerel spoils quickly, so unless it arrives at the sushi bar live, it is served cured, not raw. In Japan cured mackerel is referred to as *shime saba*. It is used widely in pressed sushi (*oshizushi*) and stick sushi (*bouzushi*). It is also used in sashimi and *nigiri*, often garnished with grated ginger and green onion and accompanied by ponzu sauce to balance out the taste.

Mackerel is widely available year-round but is at its peak during the winter.

Substitution: Spanish mackerel (*sawara*) is available year-round but is best during the summer.

Red Snapper (*Ma Dai*)

Some consider red snapper to be the king of the white-fleshed fish because its flavor is so delicate. It can be served two ways: with and without skin. For *nigiri*, it is customary for the belly side to be served skin-off, to enhance the sweet flavor of the fish. For sashimi and *chirashi*, the backside of the fillet can be seared with hot water for added texture and flavor.

Different species of snappers are widely available; in Japan they are referred to as *tai*. Red snapper is referred to as *ma dai* (true snapper). *Ma dai* comes from Japan and is available year-round but is at its peak during the spring months, when the fish have developed a nice fat content.

Substitutions: sea bream (in Europe in season from June to December); porgy (in North America in season from September to May); striped bass (available year-round from the Atlantic coast of North America); local snappers.

Salmon (*Sake*)

Salmon is by far the most popular fish ordered at Western sushi bars. Its mild and familiar flavor, bright color and semi-soft texture make it a great choice for anyone who may be a bit wary of trying raw fish for the first time. In Japan salmon is not usually eaten raw; it is often grilled with salt and eaten for breakfast.

Salmon is used for sashimi, *nigiri* and *maki*. At the sushi bar, salmon is typically cured in salt for about one hour before use to draw out moisture and any fishy flavor. It may also be rinsed in rice vinegar to kill any bacteria and remove its fishy odor.

To lessen the risk of parasites (although it doesn't eliminate it entirely), we recommend using farm-raised salmon (which spend their whole lives in the ocean) for raw preparations. Wild salmon can be used for cooked preparations (unless you know it has been commercially frozen, in which case it should be fine for raw use).

Most of the salmon you find at supermarkets that is suitable for sushi will be Atlantic farm-raised salmon, unless you're lucky enough to live in the Pacific Northwest, where fresh local wild salmon are more readily available.

Wild salmon grow up in the ocean and are caught when they return to the rivers to mate. These young salmon have a very high fat content and a lighter-colored meat. The fatty meat is sweeter and has no fishy scent. It contains 20 to 30% more body fat than mature salmon, which is similar to tuna belly (*otoro*). Wild young salmon are a delicacy, and quite expensive because they are not readily available.

The following six varieties of salmon can be used for sushi, but when in season (May to September), wild king salmon is preferred for its richer flavor:

- **Atlantic salmon:** fatty, lighter orange meat; available summer to fall
- **Pacific salmon:** large, deep orange colored meat; available farm-raised year round
- **Chinook or Copper River king salmon:** largest variety and best quality; available May to September
- **Sockeye salmon:** available wild in the summer through early fall from the Pacific Northwest, Alaska, Canada and Russia; its lean, deep orange meat is often used for canned salmon
- **Coho salmon:** chubby, deep orangey pink meat; available July to October; popular for smoking
- **Chum salmon:** light orange meat; less desired because the fish are leaner and less oily; used for salmon roe (*ikura*); available late summer to spring from the Pacific Northwest to Alaska

Wild salmon are also available in Japan. In spring, wild cherry salmon (*sakura masu*) from the Hokkaido area is available. Because it is small in size and found in rivers, it is also referred to as a trout. A rare delicacy in Japan available in the fall, *keiji* salmon are young, underdeveloped salmon that follow adults from the ocean back to the river; only one or two out of every 10,000 salmon caught are *keiji*.

Substitutions: sea trout; rainbow trout; New Zealand farmed sea trout or king salmon

Tuna (*Maguro*)

Tuna is one of the most popular fish for sushi (sashimi and *maki*), but this wasn't always the case. Before refrigeration was invented, tuna had to be eaten close to its source because its high fat content caused it to spoil quickly.

Different types of tuna can be found all over the world in all seasons. Five main species of tuna are used to make sushi: bluefin tuna (*hon maguro*), bigeye tuna (*mebachi maguro*), yellowfin tuna (*kihada maguro*), albacore tuna (*bincho maguro*) and skipjack tuna (*katsuo*). Bluefin tuna is the most prized for the beautiful texture of its meat and the various lean and fatty cuts provided by the fish.

Recently there has been much talk about the overfishing of tuna. Using tuna (or other fish, for that matter) that is in season and caught in local waters helps to promote sustainability. A true sushi chef uses fish caught in local waters—this is the best way to utilize our oceans and seas.

Farm-raised options are now being used to increase the supply of tuna, as well as other types of fish. At Kinki University in Japan, breeders are successfully farming bluefin tuna from the egg stage. *Kindai* tuna, as these tuna are called, are raised naturally in free-floating pens and fed the same types of fish or squid they would eat in the wild.

Tuna Cuts for Sushi

Tuna has three cuts of meat that are used for sashimi, *nigiri* and *maki*. These cuts are delineated by their fat content: lean (*akami*), medium-fat (*chutoro*) and fatty (*otoro*). The fatty cuts of tuna are often the prized pieces in a sushi meal.

The lean red meat (*akami*) found along the backside of tuna loins can be enjoyed either as sashimi or *nigiri*. It can also be rolled into tuna or spicy tuna *maki*. *Akami* should have a soft texture and clean taste.

In between the back and belly loins are the medium-fatty cuts (*chutoro*), which are less fatty than the belly and not quite as lean as the backside loin. *Chutoro* is a nice blend of red meat and slightly pinkish fatty meat, with a wonderful texture and lighter taste.

The fattiest cuts—the belly (*otoro*)—are the most coveted by sushi lovers. In the early days of sushi (before refrigeration) the belly was discarded because it went bad very quickly. Only bluefin tuna has the melt-in-your-mouth *otoro*; bigeye and yellowfin tuna don't quite develop the same succulent belly cuts. Excess fatty parts can be chopped and mixed with green onion to make the luxurious *negi toro maki*.

Wild tuna is available year-round, but in North America it is best from summer to early fall. In Japan, Australia and Europe, it is best from fall to winter. Yellowfin or ahi tuna from Hawaii is available year-round.

In Japan, skipjack tuna has two seasons: spring and fall. In spring it is referred to as *ha gatsuo*, or "first of the season," when the young skipjack meat is lean and dark red. It is quite flavorful and should have a fresh, clean taste. In fall it is referred to as *katsuo*, or "returning," a reference to the period when the fish are returning from their migration. The fish will have put on more weight and developed fat; their flavor is more like medium-fat tuna (*chutoro*). *Katsuo* is prepared a bit differently than regular tuna. The loins are seared over an open flame or with a blowtorch and served as *tataki*. *Katsuo* fillet should be eaten as quickly as possible because the meat quickly turns brown. It is often served with grated ginger, chopped green onions and ponzu sauce.

Yellowtail (*Hamachi*)

Yellowtail is quickly becoming a crowd favorite at the sushi bar. The mild, non-fishy flavor of this meaty fish is easy on the palate of novice sushi eaters, and a tasty treat for experienced sushi lovers.

Yellowtail is a member of the jackfish family, which also contains amberjack (*kanpachi*). It gets its name from the yellow stripe that runs along its body.

Yellowtail may be found in the Pacific from southern California to New Zealand to Japan. In peak season one can weigh as much as 40 pounds (18 kg). In Japan, the most popular regions for harvesting yellowtail are Toyama and Niigata.

At the sushi bar yellowtail is used for sashimi, *chirashi*, *nigiri* and *maki*. We like to prepare yellowtail sashimi garnished with jalapeño, cilantro and ponzu sauce, in homage to the Peruvian dish *tiradito*, sliced raw fish popularized by Japanese immigrants to that country.

Yellowtail served in low- to mid-range sushi bars will most likely be farm-raised.

The quality and consistency of this product are great. Higher-end sushi bars may refer to yellowtail by its wild name, which can be different depending on what stage in life the fish reached. The largest wild yellowtail are called *buri*. Buri are available during the late fall and peak in winter, when the fish's oils are lighter and sweeter than at other stages (which means it is the preferred stage for sushi). The smallest yellowtail are called *wakashi*; medium yellowtail are called *warasa*. Farm-raised yellowtail from Australia and other places is available year-round.

Substitutions: amberjack (*kanpachi*), flat or summer amberjack (*hiramasa*)

Seafood and Shellfish

Clams (*Nimaigai*)

Clams are used for sashimi, *nigiri* and *gunkanmaki* and can also be added to *chirashi*. Clams are admired for their delicate and sweet taste, which pairs well with sushi rice, as well as for their texture, which can range from crunchy to chewy.

Orange Clams (*Aoyagi*)

Orange clams are known for their sweetness and crunch. The foot is used for sashimi and *nigiri*, and the abductor muscles are collected from several clams to make one *gunkanmaki*. The muscle has a more concentrated flavor and chewier texture. In Japan, orange clams are in season from winter to spring.

Substitution: quahog (also known as hard clam); available in North America year round

Geoduck (*Mirugai*)

The geoduck clam is one of the largest clams around. It features a long siphon that hangs out of the shell (this is the part of the clam we eat). The geoduck clam has a savory flavor and crunchy texture. At the sushi bar it is used for sashimi and *nigiri* and is usually accompanied by pieces of yuzu (a citrus fruit) and salt. Before it is eaten, the siphon must be peeled and the meat thinly sliced; otherwise it's too tough. Geoducks are native to the northwest of North America and are available year-round.

Crabs (*Kani*)

The sweet taste of crab complements sushi rice beautifully. Crab is used in *nigiri* and *maki*, most famously the California roll.

King Crab (*Tarabagani*)

King crab is our crab of choice for making California rolls. Of all the varieties of king crab, red king crab, which is native to Alaskan waters, is the one we prefer. They are the largest of the crabs, having a leg span of up to 8 feet (2.4 meters). King crabs have a mild flavor and a meaty texture. King crab season is only two to four weeks long during the fall, but since the catch is frozen on the boat, it is available year-round. King crab can be used in *maki* or *nigiri*.

Substitution: snow crab (also available frozen year-round).

Soft-Shell Crab (*Sofuto Sheru Kurabu*)

Soft-shell crab is used to make the popular spider roll (see page 235). Soft-shell crabs are blue crabs that have recently molted, rendering their bodies soft and almost entirely edible. To maintain the soft shell, fresh crabs must be eaten within two days of being pulled from the water. Their season runs from May to September, but because of their popularity, frozen soft-shelled crab can be found at most sushi bars year-round. Typically they are served fried to give them crunch; they have the same delicate, sweet flavor as blue crabs, which aren't used for sushi.

Octopus (*Tako*)

Octopus is used in sashimi and *nigiri*, but only the arms are used (raw or blanched).

Raw octopus sashimi is fairly bland and must be very thinly sliced so it is not too chewy. For *nigiri*, octopus is massaged and poached to improve both the texture and flavor (as you chew the cooked octopus, an umami flavor is said to be released). The suckers have a crunchy texture that adventurous eaters enjoy; these can be collected and served in *gunkanmaki*. Octopus live all over the world and are available year-round.

Scallops (*Hotate*)

Scallops are prized for their soft texture and sweetness. They are butterflied for *nigiri* and sliced thinly for sashimi. Scallops reside in all the world's oceans and are also widely farmed, which means they are available year-round. Farm-raised and wild scallops taste the same; the only difference is in the color of their shells. Wild scallops are white because the sand they move around in rubs off their coloring.

Sea Urchin (*Uni*)

Sea urchin is one of the delicacies of the sea and said to be the closest expression of the flavor of the ocean. They are creamy and rich, with a melting texture. The edible portion is often mistakenly referred to as the roe—it is actually the gonads of both male and female urchins.

Sea urchin is usually served as *gunkanmaki* (page 155), because it needs help to stay on the rice. Before the invention of *gunkanmaki*, sea urchin was used only in *chirashi* or sashimi. A few drops of soy sauce are all that's needed for seasoning.

Sea urchins are available year-round but are at their peak during the summer, when the urchins are getting ready to mate and the gonads are at their largest. The best sea urchins are considered to come from coastal California, Maine, British Columbia, New Brunswick and Japan.

Shrimp (*Ebi*)

Shrimp is eaten raw as sashimi or *nigiri*, but it is more often poached to medium-rare (see page 82) to enhance its natural sweetness and improve its texture. Traditionally, the kuruma shrimp was used in sushi, but that species is now rare and expensive and so is seldom seen outside Japan. The smaller black tiger shrimp is now most commonly used. In the same genus as kuruma shrimp, it is smaller and not as tasty—however, it is abundant. Tiger shrimp are found in East Africa, South Asia, Southeast Asia, the Philippines and Australia, and they are considered an invasive species in the Gulf of Mexico and the eastern United States. They are widely farmed and available year-round.

Squid (*Ika*)

The Japanese account for 40% of the world's squid consumption. Squid is chewier than most other fish, but it's said that the more you chew, the more sweet flavor you release. Only the mantle of the squid is used for sushi and sashimi. Squid is eaten raw in sashimi and *nigiri* and cooked in preparations such as squid tempura and grilled squid. For sashimi, intricate patterns are cut into the mantle (pages 127 to 133) in order to make it less chewy. For *nigiri*, squid is scored so that it lies on the sushi rice better (see page 135). Squid is often accompanied by shiso and grated ginger. Squid are found in every ocean; peak season is spring to summer.

Roe

Flying Fish Roe (*Tobiko*)

The tiny eggs of the flying fish have a pleasing crunchy texture and nutty, salty taste (when unflavored). They are used for *chirashi* and *gunkanmaki* and on the inside and outside of *maki*. The highest-grade eggs are served unflavored and in their natural orange color. Lower grades are often colored and flavored with other ingredients, such as wasabi (green), squid ink (black) and beet juice (red). The different colors can be used separately or combined for a rainbow effect. Flying fish roe is available year-round and is packaged in the same manner as caviar.

Salmon Roe (*Ikura*)

The large orange eggs of salmon have a strong fishy flavor that is usually toned down by the addition of quail egg yolk or cucumber. Salmon roe is prepared by soaking the eggs in soy sauce and sake to remove some of the strong flavor and some of the stickiness. Both Atlantic and Pacific salmon are used for their roe, but Pacific salmon have larger eggs with a stronger flavor. Salmon roe can be used only in *chirashi* or *gunkanmaki*, because it needs a little help to stay on the rice.

Resources

A great chef is always on top of his or her *mise en place*. This is a culinary term meaning "everything in its place." By "everything" we mean ingredients, equipment and the knowledge and mindset to proceed with what you are doing. What follows is a list of our go-to resources that we think you will find helpful.

Seafood
Blue Marine Seafood:
www.bluemarineseafood.com
Browne Trading Company:
www.brownetrading.com
Catalina Offshore Products:
http://catalinaop.com
Island Seafoods:
www.islandseafoods.com
The Local Catch:
http://thelocalcatch.com/seafood-online

Sustainability
Blue Ocean:
www.blueocean.org/seafoods
Environmental Defense Fund:
http://seafood.edf.org
FishWatch: www.fishwatch.gov/index.htm
International Seafood Sustainability Foundation: http://iss-foundation.org
Marine Stewardship Council:
www.msc.org/cook-eat-enjoy/fish-to-eat
Seafood Watch: www.seafoodwatch.org/
seafood-recommendations/sushi
World Wildlife Foundation:
http://wwf.panda.org/what_we_do/
how_we_work/conservation/marine/
sustainable_fishing/sustainable_seafood/
seafood_guides

Japanese Groceries
Japan Super: www.japansuper.com
Marukai eStore:
www.marukaiestore.com
Mitsuwa Marketplace:
www.mitsuwa.com
Nijaya Market: www.nijiya.com
Rakuten Global Market:
http://global.rakuten.com

Housewares and Tableware
Akazuki: www.akazuki.com/collections/
japanese-tableware
Korin: http://korin.com/Tableware_2
Mutual Trading Company:
www.mtckitchen.com
Shop Japan: www.shopjapan.ca

Japanese Cutlery
Chef Knives to Go:
www.chefknivestogo.com
Chubo Knives: www.chuboknives.com
Cutlery and More: www.
cutleryandmore.com/japanese-knives-list
Hocho Knife: www.hocho-knife.com
Japanese Chef's Knife:
http://japanesechefsknife.com
Japanese Knife Imports:
www.japaneseknifeimports.com
Korin: http://korin.com

References

Books

Alford, Jeffrey, and Naomi Duguid. *Seductions of Rice*. New York: Artisan, 2003.

Andoh, Elizabeth. *Washoku: Recipes from the Japanese Home Kitchen*. Berkeley, CA: Ten Speed, 2005.

Barber, Kimiko. *The Japanese Kitchen: A Book of Essential Ingredients with 200 Authentic Recipes*. Lanham, MD: Kyle, 2004.

Barber, Kimiko, and Hiroki Takemura. *Sushi Taste and Technique*. New York: DK, 2002.

Berkowitz, Roger, and Jane Doerfer. *The New Legal Sea Foods Cookbook*. New York: Broadway, 2003.

Dekura, Hideo, Brigid Treloar and Ryuichi Yoshii. *The Complete Book of Sushi*. Boston, MA: Periplus, 2004.

Elliot, Jeffrey, and James P. DeWan. *Complete Book of Knife Skills: The Essential Guide to Use, Techniques & Care*. Toronto: Robert Rose, 2010.

Hisamatsu, Ikuko, and Yasunori Komatsu. *Tsukemono: Japanese Pickling Recipes*. Tokyo: JOIE, 2005.

Hosking, Richard. *A Dictionary of Japanese Food: Ingredients & Culture*. Rutland, VT: Charles E. Tuttle, 1996.

Imatani, Aya. *Sushi: The Beginner's Guide*. New York: Imagine, 2009.

Jackson, C. J., ed. *Seafood: How to Buy, Prepare, and Cook the Best Sustainable Fish and Seafood from around the World*. New York: DK, 2011.

Kamimura, Yasuko. *Sushi-Making at Home*. Tokyo: Graph-sha, 1997.

Kawasumi, Ken. *The Encyclopedia of Sushi Rolls*. Tokyo: Graph-sha, 2001.

Matsuhisa, Nobu, and Kiyomi Mikuni. *Dashi and Umami: The Heart of Japanese Cuisine*. London: Cross Media, 2009.

Morimoto, Masaharu. *Morimoto: The New Art of Japanese Cooking*. New York: DK, 2007.

Nagashima, Hiroshi, and Kenji Miura. *The Decorative Art of Japanese Food Carving: Elegant Garnishes for All Occasions*. Tokyo: Kodansha International, 2009.

Nozaki, Hiromitsu, and Kate Klippensteen. *Japanese Kitchen Knives: Essential Techniques and Recipes*. Tokyo: Kodansha International, 2009.

Peterson, James. *Fish & Shellfish*. New York: Morrow, 1996.

Pollinger, Ben, and Stephanie Lyness. *School of Fish*. New York: Gallery, 2014.

Seaver, Barton. *For Cod & Country*. New York: Sterling Epicure, 2011.

Shimizu, Kikuo. *Edomae Sushi: Art, Tradition, Simplicity*. Tokyo: Kodansha International, 2011.

The Sushi Menu Book. Tokyo: Ikeda Shoten, 2008.

Sweetser, Wendy. *The Connoisseur's Guide to Fish & Seafood*. New York: Sterling, 2009.

Tourondel, Laurent, and Andrew Friedman. *Go Fish: Fresh Ideas for American Seafood*. Hoboken, NJ: John Wiley, 2004.

Tsuji, Shizuo, and Mary Sutherland. *Japanese Cooking: A Simple Art*. Tokyo: Kodansha International, 2011.

Yoshii, Ryuichi. *Sushi*. Boston: Periplus, 1998.

Websites

FishWatch US Seafood Facts: www.fishwatch.org

Japanese Angler's Secrets: www.anglers-secrets.com

NOAA Fisheries: www.nmfs.noaa.gov

Safina Center at Stony Brook University: http://safinacenter.org

Seafood Watch: www.seafoodwatch.org

Sushi Encyclopedia: www.sushiencyclopedia.com

Sushi Monsters: www.sushimonsters.com

True World Foods – Tsukiji Express: www.trueworldfoods.com

US Food and Drug Administration: www.fda.gov

WWF Sustainable Seafood Guides: http://wwf.panda.org

Acknowledgments

Writing a book of this scope is a tremendous undertaking and takes far more people than the names you see on the cover to shepherd it to your bookshelf. We'd like to thank Bob Dees of Robert Rose for the idea to write this book and the faith he placed in us to do it, as well as for the countless shared meals and bottles of wine. Thanks as well to our editors, Judith Finlayson (an amazing author in her own right) and Tracy Bordian—without their patience (top priority for working with us), knowledge and ability to pull what was needed from us, this book would simply not exist. Gillian Watts (working with Jeffrey for the second time) handled copy editing, proofreading and indexing. Kevin Cockburn and Joseph Gisini (also a repeat) from PageWave Graphics handled design and layout. The photography was done by the immensely talented Andrew Scrivani (andrewscrivani.com—we dare you to scroll through this site and not leave hungry), whose skills behind the lens make you feel as if you can eat the photographs. Hugh Jernigan and Devon Knight, who made the weeks of shooting pass quickly and stress-free, assisted Andrew and us.

From Jeffrey

When Bob first approached me about writing a book on sushi, the first and only person who came to mind to co-write was my friend and fellow knife fanatic Robby Cook. In a city with hundreds of sushi chefs, he has been my favorite for years. My wife and I got engaged sitting at the sushi bar in front of him. His knowledge and skills are unsurpassed in New York City (or any other city for that matter). I'm glad he came on board, and that his employer allowed him the flexibility to write. I'm also thankful that he has nicer-looking—and more skilled—hands than mine (his hands appear in the photos in this book).

I would like to thank the folks at Miyabi Premium Japanese Cutlery, Zwilling J.A. Henckels, Staub, Korin Japanese Trading, and Zojirushi for their generosity with some of the best equipment a cook could ever want to use.

I would also like to thank the folks responsible for my love of fish: Chef Corky Clark, head of Fish Kitchen at the Culinary Institute of America, as well as Eric Ripert and Gilbert LeCoze (R.I.P.) of Le Bernardin. These people taught me to respect fish and seafood and to allow their natural flavors to speak for themselves. I'd like to thank my parents, Sharon and Stuart, for not batting an eye when I said I wanted to go to culinary school.

Most important, I want to thank my beautiful wife, Jill Sloane—my partner in the kitchen and in life—who has supported and encouraged me in the writing of this book and in everything else that I do.

From Robby

First and foremost, BIG thanks to Jeffrey Elliot for the opportunity to participate in this amazing project and asking me to join him in writing this book.

Thank you to Chef Masaharu Morimoto for giving me the opportunity of a lifetime and believing in me enough to run your sushi bar since 2008. Thank you for encouraging me throughout my career to keep learning, be creative and understand the foundations of sushi, but also to think outside the box.

Thanks to Ariki Omae for all the spectacular dishes you've made over the years (and continue to make) for my guests, allowing me free moments to regroup during the course of a meal. Thanks as well for allowing me to ransack your *mise en place* (ingredients) constantly and to bounce ideas off you. You are a true badass!

BIG thanks to my sushi crew for all the support! You guys are top-notch!

Thanks to all the chefs I've worked with, past and present, who have influenced my career: Jamison Blankenship, Makoto Okuwa, Yoshinori Ishii, Osamu Iino, Josh DeChellis, Matt Hudak, and the entire sous-chef crew at Morimoto for helping to keep the sushi bar tight.

I would like to thank my parents, Steve and Patty, for allowing and helping me to attend sushi and culinary schools. Without your help I wouldn't be where I am today. Thanks to my sister, Nicole, for your constant support and spreading the word of my sushi.

Most important, thanks to my lovely wife, Mio Nagumo, for your undying support and encouragement, and for enduring my crazy sushi-chef lifestyle.

Thank you to my wife's parents, Kenji and Hiromi Nagumo, for showing me your home country of Japan all these years. The rice your family harvests will always have a place at my sushi bar.

A special thank-you my longtime and dear friends April Beiter Sonksen and Heather Higgins Williams, who have supported me since day one, helping me get my feet on the ground and running here in NYC (a.k.a. letting me crash at their apartment and live with them).

A BIG shout-out to my homie and friend Cliff Cho, a.k.a. DJ Seoul, and the Direct Drive crew for their constant support and promotion of me and my sushi, always spreading the word of "tunaFase" sushi!

A HUGE shout-out to Goldie and the Metalheadz family for inspiring me to stay creative, stay fresh, stay true to myself and think of the future yet still remember my past. Much love, G.

I would also like to thank all my purveyors for helping with this project and for their donations, deliveries and support.

Thank you to Korin Japanese Trading for supplying all the equipment and plateware for the photo shoot.

Many thanks to Saori Kawano for your constant support and the beautiful eel knife—it will be in my collection forever. Thanks as well to Mitsuko Muramatsu for all your help and support on this project.

Thank you to Mark Shinohara and Yama Seafood for delivering fish for the photo shoot. Thanks as well for all your support and help over the years—especially when I forget to order things (it happens).

Thank you to Chie Asai Yokoyama, Akira Nishijima and Eiwa Marine Products at Tsukiji Market, Tokyo, for sourcing the best-quality seafood day in and day out. *Arigato gozaimasu.*

Thank you to Adam Tu and True World Foods for delivering fish, vegetables and specialty products needed for the photo shoot.

A special thank you to Minkyung Choi for the use of her one-of-a-kind handmade plateware. It provides a unique flavor and style to the photographs in this book. *Kamsahamnida!*

Index

T

U

V

W

Y

Index of Japanese Terms

Library and Archives Canada Cataloguing in Publication

Elliot, Jeffrey, author
   The complete guide to sushi & sashimi : includes 625 step-by-step photographs / Jeffrey Elliot & Robby Cook.

Includes index.
ISBN 978-0-7788-0520-5 (wire-o)

   1. Sushi. 2. Cooking, Japanese. 3. Cookbooks.
I. Cook, Robby, 1979–, author II. Title. III. Title: Complete guide to sushi and sashimi.

TX724.5.J3E44 2015   641.5952   C2015-903914-2